COST
ACCOUNTING
CONCEPTS
for
NONFINANCIAL
EXECUTIVES

COST
ACCOUNTING
CONCEPTS
for
NONFINANCIAL
EXECUTIVES

Joseph Peter Simini

amacom

**A Division of
American Management Associations**

Library of Congress Cataloging in Publication Data

Simini, Joseph Peter.
  Cost accounting concepts for nonfinancial
executives.

  Includes index.
  1. Cost accounting. I. Title.
HF5686.C8S493   657'.42   76-9851
ISBN 0-8144-5421-6

First Printing

Dedication

THIS book is dedicated to four persons under whose direction I have had the good fortune to work. All four, although separated in time and professional fields, have encouraged me, have been wise mentors, and have ever remained my friends.

Bart J. Stack (dec.), who took the time to show me that industry is a vital force in America.

Chief Machinist Mate, U.S. Navy;
Senior Inspector of Naval Materiel, Bureau of Ordnance,
U.S. Navy.

Richard L. Hanlin, C.P.A., in whose firm I received my C.P.A. certificate.

Founder of Richard L. Hanlin & Co., CPAs;
retired partner in Harris, Kerr, Forster Co., CPAs.

Roy C. Hall, J.D., who gave me my first full-time university teaching appointment.

Former Dean of College of Business Administration,
University of San Francisco;
Attorney.

Richard E. Mulcahy, S.J., Ph.D., who encouraged me to become a good teacher and a writer.

Former Dean of College of Business Administration,
University of San Francisco;
Professor of Economics, University of San Francisco.

Preface

THE title of this book, *Cost Accounting Concepts for Nonfinancial Executives,* was deliberately chosen from the start to consciously focus my direction toward the user of accounting data for controlling the enterprise he manages. This is *not* an accounting book for the accountant to use as a guide, although he might well give this book to a nonaccounting manager who wants to understand accounting concepts.

Management often lets the accountant prepare figures, statements, analyses, and other items as the accountant sees fit. After all, the accountant knows his craft and that is what he is paid for. But these accounting-oriented presentations may not be exactly what management needs. If the manager has no knowledge of the accounting concepts, he may not know what kind of report will best present the data he needs.

It is hoped that after reading this book, the manager can communicate much better with the accountant in the firm. Perhaps together they can then discover new and better ways of data presentation that will make the accountant a more meaningful contributor to management. This will give the manager more time for planning and decision making, because the accountant has given him data that are oriented to his specific managerial functions.

The reader should be aware that the content of financial statements for *publication* is undergoing review by the accounting profession and by various professional and governmental bodies. Therefore, a company's financial statements prepared in the future to satisfy the requirements for public presentation may not use some of the concepts presented herein, or may use them in some years and not be allowed to use them in other years. However, for internal management procedures to control an enterprise, the accountant may apply selected concepts in preparing figures, statements, and analyses that will be most useful to management.

My thanks go to those who over the years have given me the opportunity to teach cost accounting; to the students who studied the material and brought good questions and discussion material into the classroom and my office; and to the American Management Associations and the National Association of Accountants for inviting me to appear as a speaker in their various programs.

A word of thanks is also due Ms. Jean Rice, who assisted in the preparation of the manuscript, and my wife, Marcelline, who so generously let me steal from our time together the hours necessary to prepare this book.

The ideas contained herein are generally found in standard textbooks on cost and managerial accounting. The organization is what I consider most logical for the intended reader. The expository style of prose makes the material, in my opinion, easier for the nonaccountant to read and enjoy. Any errors and omissions in the book are my own.

Joseph Peter Simini

Contents

1

Introduction

ENTERPRISES are established and operated by people for some specific purpose. Unfortunately, the persons in charge of an enterprise or a section of an enterprise do not always have a clear understanding of its purposes and their own responsibilities within it. Too often they are unsure about just how they fit in and which of their functions relate to those of other persons in the enterprise. Usually, this situation is caused by a lack of communication within the enterprise.

One of the communication channels in business is the accounting system. The accounting section should be a scorekeeper for the enterprise, and it satisfies this obligation by reporting to responsible parties the results of their respective operations. This reporting system can do much to clarify or muddle this communication process. The basic function of this book is to help put the reader, who is not an accounting manager, in a better position to understand what the accountant does and what he can do (if he is motivated to improve communications within the enterprise), and to give the manager a better knowledge of the accounting function so that he can ask the accountant for the operating information that the manager needs.

Although this book is production-oriented, these principles of accounting information apply as well in the nonproduction areas of

1

research and development, sales, advertising, promotion, and other departments where the intermediate or end results may well be intangible benefits to the business rather than additions to inventories. If the reader is able to see the interrelationship of accounting with the tangible results of the production process, the transfer to the nontangible areas will be much easier.

THE FUNCTION OF MANAGEMENT

Management has the responsibility of taking capital, assembling resources, and establishing an organization to use those resources to provide goods or services consumers want, and to return a fair return to the investors. You may say, "I know all that—so what else is new?" The author has cause to believe that numerous management people have never seen *and thought about* such a statement of management responsibilities.

It is not easy to get capital without having a plan to return it, if borrowed, or to show how the investor can get an adequate return. In the cases of securing loans or equity capital, management does communicate hopes and plans to the lender or investor. The lending agencies and regulatory bodies ask—in fact, demand—that management put into written form its proposals for capital acquisition, use, and repayment.

Once the money is in hand, management allocates these monies to plant, labor, material, plant services, sales services, and other activities to secure maximum utilization of capital employed. Note the use of the phrase *maximum utilization of capital employed.* In the short run, profits may be low because the company is in a development stage, building a more solid base for future profitability.

Management is the control of an enterprise through people. Therefore, an understanding of the functions of the business, the interrelationships of these functions, and the principles of selection and evaluation of people who fill positions of responsibility is important. If the manager has accounting data on the operating performance of the enterprise, he can evaluate the work of his subordinates.

Management must provide those goods and services the consumers want, not what the company wants to give the consumer. This implies that management will either discover the consumers' demands or will create a demand for the product or service produced, or do both. Many companies fail to hear the consumer express his demands. The "consumer" is not a static mass, but a dynamic collection of persons whose needs and desires change over time. The highly successful business is the one that anticipates (or creates) the changes in consumer demand and then is prepared to deliver when the consumer shows up to buy.

What is a fair return to the investor? To attempt to define this as a percentage is, in the opinion of the author, a mistake. Rather, one must measure a satisfactory rate of return on investment, taking into consideration the price of money (interest rates), state of the economy (local, national, and international), the trend of the industry, availability and price of labor and material resources, and other factors. To use an inflexible formula to measure return on investment (ROI) does a disservice to those who are attempting to understand the enterprise and to evaluate it. Some communication and evaluation of the intangible company dimensions should be made by those who present data to management, investors, lenders, and other interested parties.

Another word of caution: All costs must be recovered before profit can be realized. Deferring a cost simply changes the timing of the profitability; reallocating the cost over segments merely changes segment profitability figures. In neither case is the cost less nor the total profit higher as viewed from the standpoint of the total firm over its total life.

Management, then, must establish from various sources the factors of business activity and fashion them into a rationally integrated, smooth-functioning organization; it must discover and supply the demands of consumers, and keep the lenders and investors happy. The good manager has a lot of work to do and cannot rest on past laurels because the dynamics of the marketplace make the fine tuning for yesterday's solutions inadequate for the situation today and wholly inappropriate for the challenges of tomorrow.

ORGANIZATION OF AN ENTERPRISE

The enterprise is operated by people who have assigned tasks. This requires that a study be made of the functions to be performed within the enterprise, that the size of the functional areas be defined, that the relationships among the areas be determined, and that a system of monitoring the organization be established. When this study has been made, an organizational chart and manual can be developed, and assignments can be given to competent personnel to perform the function necessary for maximum enterprise success.

People are the movers in business. The most elaborate industrial complex will produce nothing until people decide it must produce. People decide the product line; the product specifications; the extent and penetration of markets; the trade-off between profit and social responsibility, and between profit and research effort; and many similar decisions. That is, people determine business policies and practice. The organization, then, becomes a reflection of its leadership.

Business leaders should define what the business is to be, and should then study the functions to be performed. Should the enterprise make all the parts, or should it specialize in making most of the parts and subcontract some highly technical aspects to others; or should it assemble only, leaving production to other firms? Should the enterprise include the whole distributive area (sales, market research, market development, advertising, etc.), or should it use outside specialists for some of these functions? There are many options open to the leaders of a business, and they must decide which of the options they intend to pursue. This does not mean that at a later date they cannot select another set of options. A dynamic organization needs to be able to adjust to new conditions and new opportunities.

In any specified period of time, the enterprise must be large enough to perform its mission, but it should not be so dedicated to a single objective that it improperly ties up resources needed elsewhere in the enterprise. The business leader must determine the size of the enterprise and its sales potential. Here he must not be absolute ("We expect to sell $8.5 million," or "We expect to have 12 percent of the market"); rather, he should define the goals in more general terms expressed as ranges ("We expect to sell $8 to $9 million," or "We expect to have 10 to 14 percent of the market"). The latter expression of sales goal will still permit the manager to determine size of the enterprise and allow latitude for some expansion of effort. A range of sales objective, rather than an absolute one, reserves some of the resources to achieve this expandability, thus prudentially recognizing that resource allocation is a necessary function of management.

The business leader must also determine the relationships among the functional areas. He need not rethink business enterprise philosophy from the beginning, but he must clearly state where each subgroup fits in the organization and which functional area has priority. For example, can a salesman make a commitment to a customer for a delivery date of a special item, thereby binding the production manager to reschedule his program of production? There is no definitive answer because in some circumstances this commitment would be correct, but in other circumstances it would be incorrect. The business leader, in properly defining relationships, sets the policy that is best for the enterprise as a whole at this stage of its existence. In the future this policy may be changed for the betterment of the enterprise, but by then the relationships also will change.

The business leader must also establish a method whereby the organization can be monitored, to see that it is performing as it is supposed to perform. Standards of performance must be developed and communicated to the operating personnel. Methods of collecting data to be used in comparing performance to standards must be set up, and reports should be developed and distributed to the proper individuals so that they know how well they have performed, and what they must still do to achieve the results expected of them. Some measures are numerical in nature (ROI, earnings per share, gross profit margin, etc.) and are the result of normal data collection, especially in the accounting area. Other measures are personnel-oriented (evaluation of the effectiveness of information retrieval, evaluation of the handling of customer complaints, etc.) and need some interpretive rating scale so that a special data collection system can be established to evaluate performance on a regular basis and report it to the proper company officials.

The organization chart is a visual portrayal of company positions and their relationships. It helps the person looking at the chart to quickly see the company structure. It shows the lines of authority (line positions) and consultancy (staff positions) in the organization. But it is often so sketchy that the viewer must interpret it himself and deduce what the functions really are. Because it is on paper, it assumes authoritativeness and tends to say, "This is definitive." In the author's opinion, every organization chart should include names and pictures of incumbents in the various positions (assuring at least that changes will be made as incumbents change). Moreover, the organization chart should be carried down into the lower levels of the organization to insure recognition of those at the lower levels and present a better understanding of the organization as a whole.

Along with the organization chart should be an organization manual describing the various positions, thereby eliminating individual interpretation as to what each position is. The preparation of the manual will require a more detailed analysis of organization operations, and will identify the relationships of the functions within it. This detailed analysis may reveal overlapping responsibility assignments, which should be resolved by elimination of the overlap. Also, the analysis may reveal unassigned areas of responsibility which need to be assigned to someone particularly. Overlapping responsibilities should be avoided, to prevent duplication of effort and conflicting orders as well as to deter the tendency of some persons to assume so many functions and amass excessive authority to the extent that their operations become uncontrollable. Unassigned areas should be avoided because either the functions will not be accomplished or they will be taken over by individuals who are not entirely qualified to perform the tasks left unassigned.

People are the prime movers in an enterprise. These people must be organized into a functioning team by determining what must be done, how large the organization should be to meet its objectives, and what the interrelationship between the functional areas should be. A system of developing standards of performance and collecting data to measure and review performance must be instituted. The organization should be defined graphically and in writing, and should be reviewed periodically and as the need arises. Then the assignment of personnel to implement the activities of the organization can be made much more selectively, thus improving the chances for successful completion of assignments.

RESPONSIBILITY ACCOUNTING

As has been stated previously, some of the measures of performance are numerical in nature, and therefore the accounting system is the source generally used to provide the necessary data. Although accounting by nature collects dollar amounts, the source documents used by the accountant also show other data that can be used for performance measurement. Just as other departments in the organization are assigned functions to perform, responsibility accounting is assigned the job of collecting data by functional areas so that standards can be developed. It must also report operating results in these same functional areas so that supervisory personnel can evaluate the results of their subordinates.

Accounting has traditionally gathered and summarized financial data to present a statement of financial condition (Balance Sheet) as of the last day of the fiscal period, a statement of operational results (Statement of Income and Expense) for that fiscal period, and a statement of changes in the owners' equity (Retained Earnings Statement) over the same period. These statements are a historical presentation. There is still need to present these data in an acceptable form, and the accountant will adapt his presentation techniques to make the statements comply with the reporting requirements of the Securities and Exchange Commission, the stock exchanges, lenders, and other statement users who are authorized to demand greater detail in reports of financial data. But for public presentation the enterprise need present only a generalized data summary, since the process of collecting and summarizing data, having it audited, and preparing it for dissemination is an expensive enough process without expanding the scope of the reporting.

In the area of internal responsibility accounting, however, the accountant collects and classifies data that management needs to operate the company efficiently. The forms for presenting the data are not generally based on accepted accounting principles or on legal and institutional requirements, but are those that management can easily and rapidly interpret.

The management accountant, an accounting specialist who has as his function the development of information that management needs, is a prime mover in the revolution to expand management's thorough understanding of the enterprise. He does this by reshaping the accounting system to give the specific management-oriented data that are necessary for operational control.

Because the management accountant knows what will be collected currently, he can go into past records and develop standards of past performance that can be used as a benchmark for measuring present performance. In the transition from traditional to responsibility accounting, the accountant will find the standards to be inadequate, but he can adapt them in a relatively short period of time and develop a very useful and accurate guide.

Since source documents contain other than dollar data, the management accountant can expand the data collection system to incorporate the nonfinancial data. For example a sales invoice shows the customer (by name and address), the salesman, the various items sold by number of units and price, and the credit terms. By the use of computers and a proper designing of input format, the management accountant can not only determine the total dollar sales but can also secure total sales by sales personnel, location (by use of zip code), total number of each item sold by unit and dollar value, etc. These figures may be much more valuable in evaluating advertising efforts, changes in credit terms, etc. Here, knowledge of what management can use and the facility of computer technology can be profitably wedded to reduce overall costs of operation.

Responsibility accounting, then, can expand the data base to develop data more useful to management, can analyze past data to develop performance standards, and can assist the management of an enterprise to develop a more efficient operation.

ORGANIZATION OF THE PRODUCTION FACILITIES

It might help to visualize the production facilities by describing what is done in a plant. The *plant manager* is generally given the responsibility to combine the resources of labor, material, and capital to produce salable product. He is assisted in these tasks by people involved in the areas of personnel, materials, production, plant upkeep, transportation, and administrative services, among others. The area of personnel involves hiring, training, discharging, and evaluating plant personnel, administering labor relations and fringe-benefit programs, and operating health services. The area of materials includes purchasing, expediting deliveries, receiving and inspecting incoming materials, stockroom keeping, studying inventory movement, and storing finished goods. The area of production includes determining processes, scheduling production, routing production, and inspecting for quality control. The area of plant upkeep includes repairing and maintaining the plant and equipment, furnishing plant utilities, and the like. Transportation includes routing of materials purchased, routing of finished goods to market, and supplying internal transportation within the plant. Administrative services includes general accounting, cost accounting, safety, security, records management, and the like. The organization chart for these functions might look like Figure 1.1.

Figure 1.1   Pro forma organization chart.

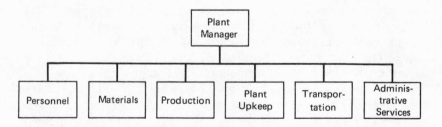

One can see, then, that operation of the plant itself involves many people whose effort and expense are not directly product-related, but who are necessary in order that the production function can operate smoothly.

COST ACCOUNTING ORGANIZATION

The cost accounting organization is a specialized section of the accounting effort which has as its function the development of the unit cost of production. It collects data from production orders, labor tickets, materials-usage tickets, and other production documents, prices these documents, and accumulates costs, assigning them to the products produced.

It is important that all plant-related costs will be finally reflected in the unit cost of the product, for purposes of bidding and cost/price determination, so that the product can be sold at a profit. However, there are activities in the plant that are related to sales or general administration. These must not be charged to unit cost but to the proper areas of the business for purposes of responsibility accounting. For example, the goods are completed, inspected, and placed in the finished goods stockroom. All costs from that point on are really distribution costs and become the responsibility of and controllable by the sales manager, who directs the outflow of products. For convenience, the goods are stored at the factory site and distribution personnel work at the factory.

The cost accountant must choose from among three methods of assigning costs to production, and this causes some confusion to the nonaccountant (and considerable debate among accountants). Each of the three methods offers an alternative.

1. Costs may be related to the production process itself, either to *job-order* cost or *process* cost.
2. Costs may be based on price because all elements of production expense fluctuate. The pricing method used may be either *historical* or *standard* costing.
3. Costs may be related to the timing of expense and may be allocated as either *absorption* or *direct* costing.

These methods are explained in Chapter 2.

The important thing for the nonaccountant to know and remember is that any one of these methods may produce different per-unit costs over a short period of time, but that total costs in the long run will be the same because all production must absorb all costs of manufacture. The different methods of cost accounting do not reduce an expenditure, once made, but merely vary the timing of converting that expenditure to an expense. The closer the plant operates to its designed capacity, and the closer it estimates the cost of goods and services, the closer it will come to the predicted profit margin in the unit sales price.

Nonaccounting managers select the method the cost accountant uses (after consultation with the accounting staff and the auditing firm). Therefore, they should be confident that their decision will not change the long-run profitability of the enterprise.

COST ACCOUNTING APPLICATION TO NONPRODUCTION FUNCTIONS

One of the real benefits to the nonaccounting manager who takes the time to master the text of this book is that he can use the production concepts to price out nonproductive activities such as sales effort, advertising, transportation, order processing, typing, and filing. He also will be better qualified to make more significant contributions to the budgeting processes within the firm. Once people in managerial positions are better informed of accounting and budgetary processes, the firm will develop a cost-saving attitude that will make it more competitive and ultimately more profitable.

2

Definition of Terms and Cost Flow

IN this chapter the terms used by management accountants (which includes cost accountants and managerial accountants) are defined to give the reader a better understanding of the accounting concepts that follow. The function of this book is not to make the reader an accountant but to give him sufficient knowledge to understand what the accountant does and how he can communicate better with the accountant so as to make greater use of the accountant in the area of cost reduction.

METHODS OF ACCOUNTING

Job-order cost accounting. This method is used when the process consists of separable units of production, such as a lot of tables (say, 50 tables). The type of production is characterized by general-purpose machinery in which the process can be stopped and the machinery changed to allow another lot to be processed through a particular machine at little or no increase in cost to either lot. This is characterized as being a more labor-intense process. A good example is the construction of four types of wooden chairs and three types of wooden tables in one plant. A lot of 50 chairs of type A can be started and then a lot of 25 tables of type M can follow. If a rush order for 30 chairs of type C comes in, it can be routed through the plant, stopping the other lots at whatever stage of production to let the rush order through.

Process cost accounting. This cost accounting method is used when the process requires continuous input of material, such as oil in a refinery. The type of production is characterized by special-purpose machinery where the process cannot be stopped or changed except at considerable cost increase. An operation of this nature is considered a capital-intense process. A good example would be a juice extraction plant, which could not be switched over to a wine-making process because it would be too costly to convert from the juice extraction machinery.

Note: In both job-order and process cost accounting the unit price is determined. In a process type of operation that is of relatively short duration (such as cooking soup for canning), job-order cost accounting should be used.

Historical cost accounting. This cost accounting method uses actual prices for the actual quantities of labor and material used for production cost. Because of alternative methods of charging material costs to production, unit prices would vary from one alternative method to another. Differing wage rates assigned to a specific task would also cause a difference in unit prices.

Standard cost accounting. The cost accounting method assumes that a product has a standard quantity of labor and material and that these elements have a standard cost. In reality, more or less units might be used than the "standard quantity" and the unit price paid might be more or less than the "standard price." This method simplifies the day-to-day costing of production and requires the collection of variances for both labor and material sometime during the fiscal period. The analysis of these variances can be a valuable tool in reducing overall production (and therefore per-unit) costs.

Note: In both historical and standard cost accounting, nondirect costs are charged to production at a predetermined burden or overhead rate. Either historical or standard costs can be used with job-order or process cost accounting.

Absorption versus Direct Cost Accounting

Absorption cost accounting is a method that includes all nondirect product costs in the burden or overhead rate, thereby causing unit cost of uncompleted goods on hand at the year's end to be higher than under the direct costing method.

Direct cost accounting is a method that separates nondirect product costs into two kinds: one that occurs without relation to production (property taxes, insurance on plant, etc.) and another that varies with production. The burden or overhead rate includes only the latter types of expense, thereby causing unit costs of uncompleted goods on hand at year's end to be lower than under the absorption costing method. The nondirect product costs that occur without relation to production are expenses in the fiscal period incurred. (*Note:* The Cost Accounting Standards Board [see Appendix C] has recommended against the continuing use of direct costing.)

Direct costing and absorption costing differ in the timing of cost charges. Although the two methods are independent of each other, certain aspects can be related, as shown in Figure 2.1. It can also be seen that selection of one system in each group gives the possibility of eight different cost systems.

Figure 2.1   Variety of cost accounting systems.

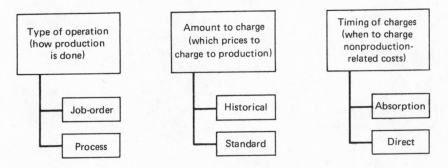

Absorption costs are the costs of the period that (although accumulated without regard to the production output) will be allocated to production and will be part of the cost assigned to the year's end inventory.

Direct costs may be defined as costs incurred regardless of production volume. They are costs that go on at some given level (usually called "overhead") and are similar to fixed costs. The proponents of direct costing charge these costs to the period in which they are incurred. The reasoning is that they do not vary with production and should therefore not be inventoried.

An illustration may help us here: Assume direct labor of $500,000, direct material of $300,000, fixed costs allocable to production (factory

14

overhead) of $250,000, and other fixed costs of $200,000. Assume further that of 50,000 units completed, 40,000 units are sold in the first year for $35 each ($1,400,000). Comparative income statements would appear as shown in Table 2.1. Note that the lower profit shown under direct costing at A ($400,000 − $360,000 = $40,000) is reflected in $40,000 less year's end inventory at B under direct costing ($250,000 − $210,000 = $40,000). In the next year, when the remaining 10,000 units are sold, the comparative income statements would appear as listed in Table 2.2.

Table 2.1

	Direct Costing	Absorption Costing
Direct labor	$ 500,000	$ 500,000
Direct materials	300,000	300,000
Factory overhead	250,000	450,000
	$1,050,000	$1,250,000
Cost per unit	$21	$25
Sales (40,000 units)	$1,400,000	$1,400,000
Cost of sales	840,000	1,000,000
Other fixed costs	200,000	-0-
	1,040,000	1,000,000
A. Profit	$ 360,000	$ 400,000
B. Year's end inventory	$ 210,000	$ 250,000

Table 2.2

	Direct Costing	Absorption Costing
Sales	$350,000	$350,000
Less remaining inventory	210,000	250,000
Profit	$140,000	$100,000
Total profit		
First year	$360,000	$400,000
Second year	140,000	100,000
Total profit	$500,000	$500,000

The profit shown in Table 2.2 might better be described as "gross profit" because no deductions were made for selling and administrative expenses.

It can be seen that the difference in the two methods is the timing of cost and therefore a shifting of the income. No costs were reduced and no new income was generated.

If the plant operates somewhere near the middle of the relevant range and sells approximately each year's production in that year (that is, inventory levels do not change much in quantity), the difference in income under the two methods will not be large, except for the first year (where inventories are being built up) and the last year (where inventories are being sold off).

As can be seen from Figure 2.1, there are eight possible combinations of costing systems. Each plant must decide for itself which one can best communicate what the plant does. In making that choice a certain result is achieved that is different from the results achieved by the other seven. But the difference is found only in the short run; in the long run the results must be the same.

INVENTORIES

Inventory is a large part of the assets of a company, and it is easy to lose sight of the dollar volume invested. There are certain factors, to be discussed in Chapter 5, that tend to increase inventory size. A whole area called *inventory management* has been developed to control this asset.

Raw materials inventory (RM or RM Inv). This asset is the total cost of goods received from outside the plant and which have not yet entered production. The work "raw" as an adjective might conjure up things like iron ore or oil at the wellhead, but that does not apply here. Its use in this book implies parts or auxiliary materials, such as tires purchased by a car manufacturer, bathtubs by a home builder, or sheet metal by a refrigerator manufacturer. One of the problems accountants must resolve is the fluctuation of prices from purchase to purchase. How this problem is handled is also discussed in Chapter 5.

Work-in-process inventory (WIP or WIP Inv). This asset is the total cost of raw materials put into production, plus the labor used to transform the goods into *any stage* of a marketable product, plus a *fair* share of the factory overhead related to this stage of completion. Work in process forms a connecting link between processes, and a

Figure 2.2 Diagram of cost accounting flows through production.

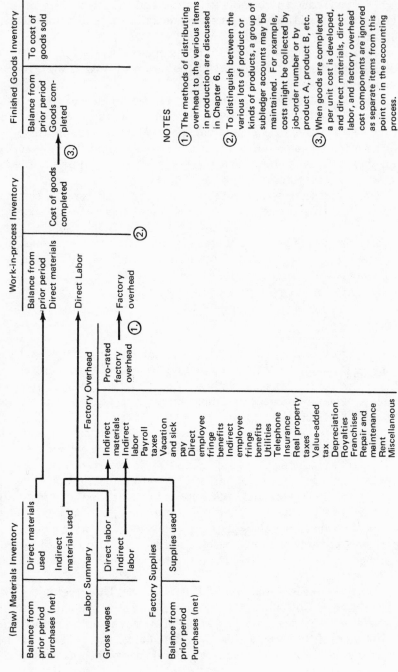

NOTES

1. The methods of distributing overhead to the various items in production are discussed in Chapter 6.

2. To distinguish between the various lots of product or kinds of products, a group of subledger accounts may be maintained. For example, costs might be collected by job-order number or by product A, product B, etc.

3. When goods are completed a per unit cost is developed, and direct materials, direct labor, and factory overhead cost components are ignored as separate items from this point on in the accounting process.

certain amount is required to serve as an interprocess buffer to keep the plant operating efficiently in the event of a breakdown of any process in the chain of production.

Finished goods inventory (abbreviated as FG or FG Inv). This asset is the total cost of raw materials put into production, plus the labor use to transform them to *completion*, plus a *fair* share of the factory overhead. These goods will have gone through the total production cycle and be ready for sale.

MATERIALS

Direct materials (DM). These are materials that are used and become an integral part of the product (for example, the fenders on a car in an assembly plant or the sheet steel in a refrigerator door). For the sake of convenience, the accountant may not account for some small items of direct materials that are part of the product, such as the glue in a book. The cost of small amounts of these items is so minor in relation to the other direct materials costs in the same period that the effort of apportioning fractional expense to the product would be greater than the value of accuracy achieved.

Indirect materials (Ind M). Materials other than direct materials (for example, factory office supplies, janitorial supplies, lubricating greases and oils for machinery, maintenance parts and supplies). This also includes the small items not charged to direct materials noted above.

In the accounting records there may be a separate account called *Factory Supplies* in which those supplies that are always overhead items are accounted for. Sometimes they are included as part of the (RAW) Materials Inventory account.

LABOR

Direct labor (DL). This item refers to the gross wage cost of labor that is directly related to production (such as the gross wage cost of the person who is installing the motor in the refrigerator, or welding the chassis, or painting the tabletop).

Indirect labor (Ind L). This expense includes all factory labor costs other than direct labor (for example, the gross wage cost of plant administration, nonproducing foremen, or stockroom clerks).

A problem arises when a person hired to produce a product is in attendance but cannot perform his work because of machine breakdown or improper scheduling. For purposes of control, this nonproductive time should be separately recorded so that the situation can be analyzed and proper measures can be taken to prevent recurrence as much as possible. Costs other than gross wages relating to labor will be discussed in the next section, "Factory Overhead." Another problem is the premium paid to the production worker for overtime and shift differential.

FACTORY OVERHEAD

All costs of operating the factory, other than direct materials and direct labor, are included in factory overhead. Among these are indirect materials and indirect labor, which were discussed in the preceding section. Other items are considered below.

Payroll taxes. These taxes are paid by the employer on the gross wages of *all* factory employees, as required by law. Workmen's compensation insurance might well be included in this item because it is an employer cost required by law.

Vacation and sick pay. This represents gross wages paid to employees who are not in attendance because they have been granted time off in accordance with company practice, union contract agreement, etc. The category might include time off for jury duty, illness, or death in the family, etc.

Direct employee fringe benefits. Employer-paid items that benefit the individual factory employee, such as the employer's share of medical and dental insurance, life insurance, or stock-purchase plans, are included in this account.

Indirect employee fringe benefits. Employer-paid items that are available to all factory employees as a group, to be used or not by an individual factory employee as he sees fit, are also considered as fringe benefits. Included in this would be the cafeteria, the parking lot, the softball league, the bowling leagues, personal enrichment programs, and similar activities.

Utilities. The cost of electricity, gas, and water used in the factory are overhead items. If general administrative, sales, or other nonfactory facilities are located at the plant site, these costs must be prorated on some equitable basis.

Telephone and communications. The costs of telephone and communication services used in the factory are also overhead. If general, sales, or other nonfactory facilities are located at the plant site, these costs must be prorated on some equitable basis.

Insurance. Insurance to cover inventory loss, fire, explosion, work stoppage, etc., that are production-related is another cost. This is charged to factory overhead in an analysis of the risk involved and the type of coverage purchased.

Real property taxes. County and city taxes on real property are also prorated if nonfactory facilities are located at the plant site.

Personal property taxes. If there are state or local taxes on personal property, they are allocated to the company unit that has control and use of the property. The valuation of personal property and rate of taxation can be so high that some companies give serious consideration to this item in choosing the original plant location or in continuing the plant at the present site.

Value-added tax. This tax has not yet been introduced on a wide scale in America, but it is levied extensively in Europe. There has been considerable discussion of this tax in Congress, and it is to the interest of business firms to examine carefully the arguments pro and con. Basically, the tax is applied to the increases in value of the product as it passes through the production and sales cycles. This cost must be passed on to the consumer. It is essentially a hidden sales tax, and must be considered in pricing procedures.

Depreciation. This is an allocation of cost less reasonable salvage value of plant assets over the economic or physical life of each asset. This will be discussed at greater length in Chapter 6.

Royalties. The cost paid to the owner of a patent for the use of that patent can be paid at a flat rate per unit produced or as a flat sum per year.

Franchises. The cost paid to the owner of a product for the privilege to produce that product is paid at a flat rate per unit produced.

Repair and maintenance. This account includes costs of repairing and maintaining the factory building (prorated if some space is used by nonfactory facilities) as well as the plant machinery and equipment.

Rent. Money paid to the landlord for use of space (prorated if some space is used by nonfactory facilities) is allocated as rent.

Miscellaneous. All other factory costs not specifically mentioned above are considered as miscellaneous expense. If any portion or item can be identified as a substantial cost, it is generally segregated for purposes of control.

QUESTIONS*

1. Classify the following uses of materials and labor as direct or indirect costs of the machine shop.

   (a) Labor spent in preparing a bid.
   (b) Paper used in preparing a bid.
   (c) Labor of machinist in making a repair part for a lathe used in production
   (d) Labor of machinist on a customer's order.
   (e) Paint used to paint plant machinery.
   (f) Steel rods used on a customer's order.
   (g) Paint used to finish a customer's order.
   (h) Paper used in production scheduling.
   (i) Labor of production scheduler.

2. A plant site includes a factory, some administrative offices, a sales office, and some shipping facilities (for shipment of completed orders to customers). Give some method of allocating the following costs:

   (a) Telephone
   (b) Rent
   (c) Heat
   (d) Electricity
   (e) Property taxes

*Answers are given at the back of the book.

3

Labor

THE cost of labor in a product is hard to estimate when looking at the product. Yet labor is a significant part of product cost in practically all cases. Without tight control, labor costs can spell the difference between success and failure of the product in the marketplace.

There are two basic types of wages for labor: those based on attendance and those paid for performance. The difficulty with labor compensation is that it is a purchase of the employee's time and as such cannot be inventoried as material can. It is paid for as time goes on, and if it is unused, or used inefficiently, it is lost forever. The problem, then, is the choice of wage type. Should the employer pay for labor by the hour, thus knowing the cost but speculating on productivity while the worker is assured of a given wage? On the other hand, should he pay by the piece or unit of work, solving the employer's productivity problem but leaving the worker unsure as to the amount of his income to some extent? A solution to this conflict is to establish some form of incentive system that will guarantee a minimum wage per hour, with increased wages as productivity goes up. The employer can hope to offset the additional per-unit labor cost by the lower overhead charges realized by increasing the number of units produced within the time schedule.

In addition to gross wages, the employer is legally obligated to pay certain taxes, premiums for social security (retirement) and medicare (medical benefits), federal and state unemployment benefits, and workmen's compensation benefits (pay for loss of time due to an on-the-job accident). To attract workers and be competitive in the labor market, the employer must often pay for other fringe benefits, such as all or part of major medical and dental insurance, group life insurance premiums, part of stock-purchase plans, all or part of retirement plans in addition to social security, and furnishing space (parking lots) or facilities (lunchrooms), or social-type activities (sports leagues, family picnics, etc.), and other employee-related items. All these labor costs must be properly classified into direct labor (used in production) and indirect labor (not used in production directly, but necessary to enable the productive process to continue efficiently).

GROSS WAGES

In wage legislation, the gross wage is the base on which taxes are computed. In many fringe benefits, it is used to determine other benefits. Not all gross wages are included in computing benefits, for two reasons: (1) The gross wage may exceed the statutory limits for taxation, thereby being taxable up to a point but not taxable beyond that point; and (2) the particular service may be tax exempt for reasons spelled out in the appropriate tax law. As will be shown later, there are different limits of gross wages for different kinds of taxes.

Time-Attendance Gross Wages

Under this method of determining gross wages the employer pays for time in attendance. This type of payment extends from the top executive to the hourly worker. In the upper echelons of business, time attendance is loosely interpreted to mean "in physical attendance" because the executive's experience and trained mind are the benefits the company wants and these attributes can be exercised anywhere and at any time. The competent executive makes the company an integral part of his life and works on company problems wherever he is at any time of day. For this he is paid a yearly or monthly salary and is not expected to follow a rigid "nine to five" schedule at the office.

Further down in the organizational structure we find monthly employees who are expected to be in attendance at their assigned place of work during the normal hours of work on the days the business is open. There is some degree of latitude generally given to supervisors to allow these employees some time off for personal reasons without loss of pay, as long as the privilege is not abused. The work to be done is accomplished either by the employee at another time (after normal business hours) or by fellow employees on a loose cooperative arrangement of give and take. The hourly employee is paid only when physically in attendance. If he takes off for personal reasons, he is not paid (except as stipulated in a contractual relationship).

Under the time-attendance method of pay the company depends on employee integrity and loyalty to the company to insure that work will be accomplished efficiently and expeditiously. However, the author and the reader both know of employees on any level who are conscious of their responsibilities to the company and do their job and more, and also know of employees who do less than is required or do it in a sloppy and slovenly manner. It is the opinion of the author that top management should identify the former and recognize him through advancement and increased compensation, and should identify the latter and reeducate him so that he will become a better employee (if this cannot be done, his employment should be terminated).

In time attendance, gross wages are easily determined. The time in attendance is multiplied by the rate. An executive under contract for $27,000 per year earns $2,250 per month. If he starts or leaves in the month, the pay is prorated on the basis of calendar days or working days, depending on company practice. If the pay period is semimonthly, the gross wages are $1,125 per pay period; if biweekly, the gross wages are $1,038.46, or 27,000/26 per pay period.

An employee whose salary is $700 per month has gross wages of $350 semimonthly; $323.08, or 12 × 700/26, biweekly; or $161.54 weekly (12 × 700/52).

Performance Gross Wages

Under this form of payment each unit of work is rated by the company and so much will be paid by the company to the worker to accomplish the task. For example, the company will post a piecework price of $2.00 to produce one unit of item A. If one worker produces 11 units of item A in a given eight-hour day, his gross wages are $22. If, however, another worker produces only eight units, his gross wages for that day are $16.

This method of pay meets many criticisms. If the average wage expected by the employee is $2.50 per hour, the first employee would be happy because he would have been paid $2.75 per hour. But the second employee would be unhappy because he would have been paid only $2.00 per hour. Obviously, this difference is caused by the piecework rate of production. However, all workers do not always expect the same wage as their coworkers. Suppose that the first employee in this example expected $3.00 per hour. Then, he would now be unhappy because he would have been paid only $2.75 per hour. In paying under a piece-rate system, therefore, employee expectations must be met, and these expectations increase proportionally with increased skill and longevity.

Another criticism of the performance base concerns time lost by an employee through no fault of his own. Suppose that the second employee in the original example produced only eight units because his machine broke down, or there were insufficient units for him to work on, and so he had to sit idle for 2 hours. His unhappiness is due to lack of opportunity to earn while his time (earning capacity) is being used and he is unpaid. The remedy for this is for the employer to keep the employee occupied during the hours in attendance by switching him to a new assignment or by paying him on a basic hourly rate when no assignment is available. For example, an employee is given an hourly rate of $2.50 (his expectation of pay) and is assigned to produce item A at $2.00 each. He works for 4 hours, and then his machine breaks down and its repair takes 2 hours. After the repair, he works for two more hours, and his total production is eight units. Now his gross wages are $21 (8 units at $2.00 each + 2 hours × $2.50 per hour). The employee is happy now, but the employer is not because each of those eight units has cost him $2.625 instead of $2.00. However, the employer can reassign the worker (to another machine), can establish a better maintenance schedule to prevent breakdowns, or can establish a better production schedule to prevent material shortage.

Another criticism is that standards of performance are not equitable when one operation is compared to another. Let us assume two tasks: Task A is rated at $1.00 per unit and task B is rated at $0.50 per unit; the expected rate of pay is $2.50 per hour. If an employee can complete 27 units of A ($27.00) in one day, but can complete only 45 units of B ($22.50) in one day with the same amount of effort on his part, then A is a "better" job than B. When disparities of this type exist, the assignment of jobs can be used unfairly to reward "pets" and to punish "troublemakers." This type of treatment has a disastrous effect on personnel when the disparity becomes wide enough and the selective assignment structures become apparent, and it doesn't take long for employees to recognize the technique.

Partly, disparity in piecework is the fault of those employees who tend to be less than honest in their effort when piecework rates are being established. Part of the fault, however, may be due to the employer if he tries to set higher than reasonable standards. Or, even if he doesn't, he may fail to impress on employees that fair standards are a two-way street: They increase the employees' checks while at the same time give the company a fair return for wages paid.

The establishment of standards should be done on a scientific basis through time-and-motion study, micromotion filming, job breakdown and analysis, and the use of universally accepted procedures. If they are generated internally, some mechanism should be set up to adjust and coordinate equitable standards between operations.

It is appropriate here to discuss the use of a suggestion system with suitable rewards. The employee who is performing a task on an extended basis often sees methods of improving his operation. Without a suggestion system, his improved method may never be revealed to management (even though the employee uses it himself). Then, if the employee is shifted to a new assignment, his replacement may use the former less efficient method.

The method of reward should be spelled out clearly and simply so that the employee can understand it. The amount of reward should be related to savings in some way (say, 25 percent of the savings in the first year). It goes without saying that suggestions should be coded in some way other than with the employee's name, to insure fair review without regard to the person involved.

One can see, then, that although piecework is a fair method of paying for work done, it has its drawbacks. Some of the objections have been satisfied by the introduction of incentive systems.

INCENTIVE SYSTEMS

Another method for computing gross wages is by use of some form of incentive plan. The purpose of these plans is to encourage an employee to produce more in a given time. The effect of this on the per-unit price of the product produced will be discussed at the end of this section.

For incentive systems to work well, the plan must be clearly stated so that the employee knows how the additional wages can be earned.

The reward for increased productivity should be paid close to the end of the period of production (for example, this week's paycheck should reflect last week's production). The standards for each different unit of production should be equitably established so that "easy" and "tough" jobs will be eliminated as much as possible. The administration of the plan at the assignment level should be fair so that all employees get an opportunity to participate. To really spur increased output, the plan should have a scaled payment system so that proportionally more is paid to employees as they produce more in a given time. The plan should guarantee that in periods when incentive work is not available, for whatever reason, the employees will be paid the regular wages in those periods.

Straight Piecework

The simplest form of incentive is straight piecework. Under this plan an employee is paid so much per unit to perform certain operations. The more he produces, the more he earns. This is effective when the employee, not the machine, can control the rate of production.

Let us assume that an employee has a pay rate of $3.50 per hour. He is assigned a job that pays 35¢ per piece where the standard production rate is ten units per hour. If he works at a normal pace, he will earn the $3.50 per hour. Sometimes he may produce more than ten units per hour; sometimes, less. If, however, he can increase his production above ten units per hour, on the average, he will earn more. For example:

        8 hours   @$3.50/hour   = $28.00
        8 hours @10/hour @35¢ each   = $28.00
        8 hours @12/hour @35¢ each   = $33.60
        8 hours @15/hour @35¢ each   = $42.00

When the employee who is adept at producing at this rate continues to make substantially more units over standard for an extended period of time, there may be efforts by the company to revise the standard (although ten units may be equitable) or other employees may try to slow him down so he will not upset the standard.

100 Percent Bonus Plan

The 100 percent plan is based on the proposition that each unit takes a given time to produce. The employee is then assigned to do the job, and the units of time are collected for units produced.

Then this is converted to gross pay by an efficiency factor (Table 3.1) or by a time factor (Table 3.2).

In Table 3.1, note that although employee A did not reach an efficiency rate of 1.0, he is still paid at the base rate. It is assumed that he worked 8 hours on this one unit. In Table 3.2, again he failed to produce 8 hours of work, but is still paid the guaranteed rate.

In this plan, as compared to straight piecework, the amount paid the employee per hour is irrelevant because the employee is measured against a standard in terms of efficiency and time. This gives flexibility so that an employee can be assigned to a job regardless of unit value (that is, an employee *must* make a given amount of money). The employee is satisfied as long as the standard is obtainable.

Another interesting use of this plan is to compensate a group of men who work as a team. They can then parcel out the assignments and police the performances within the group. The gross wages of each member are proportionately higher over the regular gross wage if a bonus is earned.

Taylor Differential Piece Rate

This system of incentive pay uses a dual system of piecework rates, one for the poorer or newer employee and another for the better or more experienced employee.

Let us assume two employees: A, a new employee, and B, an experienced employee. A's wage rate is $2.50 per hour; B's rate is $3.50 per hour, as shown in Table 3.3. Both are assigned to the same task, which has a standard of ten units per hour. The rate per piece for A is 20¢ and for B is 30¢. If each produces 80 units in one 8-hour day, then no incentive is provided. Neither A nor B has produced more than the standard 10 units per hour to earn a production bonus, and each is therefore paid the straight hourly wage. Now suppose that each produces 105 units in one day, as shown in Table 3.4. Then both employees have produced enough to get a production bonus.

Halsey Premium

Under this plan the employee is paid a percentage of the time saved over the standard rate per piece.

Let us assume a standard rate of 120 pieces per 8-hour day at a wage rate of $2.50 per hour. The employee receives as a bonus 40 percent of the time saved. The figures for three days of the week

Table 3.1 Efficiency factor method—8-hour day.

Employee	Units Produced (1)	Standard Units (2)	Efficiency Ratio (3) = (1) ÷ (2)	Base Rate (4)	Adjusted Rate (5) = (3) × (4)	Hours Worked (6)	Gross Wages (7) = (6) × higher of (4) or (5)
A	90	100	0.90	$3.00	$~~2.70~~	8	$24.00
B	100	100	1.00	3.25	~~3.25~~	8	26.00
C	110	100	1.10	~~2.75~~	3.025	8	24.20

Table 3.2 Time factor method—8-hour day (.08 hr/unit).

Employee	Units Produced (1)	Time (hrs.) per Unit (2)	Production Hours (3) = (1) × (2)	Hours Worked (4)	Base Rate (5)	Gross Pay (6) = (5) × higher of (3) or (4)
A	90	0.08	~~7.2~~	8.0	$3.00	$24.00
B	100	0.08	~~8.0~~	8.0	3.25	26.00
C	110	0.08	8.8	~~8.0~~	2.75	24.20

Table 3.3

Employee	Number Produced (1)	Rate (2)	Gross Wages (3) = (1) × (2)	Hours (4)	Base Rate (5)	Gross Wages (6) = (4) × (5)	Gross Wages (higher of (3) or (6))
A	80	$0.20	$16.00	8	$2.50	$20.00	$20.00
B	80	$0.30	$24.00	8	$3.50	$28.00	$32.00

Table 3.4

	Number Produced (1)	Rate (2)	Gross Wages (3) = (1) × (2)	Hours (4)	Base Wages (5)	Gross Wages (6) = (4) × (5)	Gross Wages (higher of (3) or (6))
A	105	$0.20	$21.00	8	$2.50	$20.00	$21.00
B	105	$0.30	$31.50	8	$3.50	$28.00	$31.50

Table 3.5

	Standard Production (1)	Actual Production (2)	Actual Over Standard (3) = (2) − (1)	Standard Time/ Unit (4)	40% of Time Saved (5) = (3) × (4) × 0.4	Actual Time Gross Wages (6) = $2.50 × 8	Bonus (7) = (5) ÷ 60 × $2.50	Gross Wages (8) = (6) + (7)
Monday	120	100	0	4 min	0	$20.00	$0	$20.00
Tuesday	120	120	0	4 min	0	20.00	0	20.00
Wednesday	120	150	30	4 min	48 min	20.00	2.00	22.00

are given in Table 3.5. On Monday this employee did not earn a bonus and is paid straight time; Tuesday, he earned just the standard; Wednesday, he exceeded the standard and receives a bonus of $2.00 for 40 percent of the time saved.

Emerson Efficiency Plan

Under this type of plan, actual production is measured against standards and then pay is made according to efficiency ratings, as follows:

Efficiency, %	Bonus, %
Up to 70	0
70–85	10
85–100	20
100–125	30
Over 125	40

Let us assume that 100 units is the standard 8-hour production day for five employees: A earns $2.50 per hour and produces 65 units; B earns $3.00 per hour and produces 111 units; C earns $2.70 per hour and produces 83 units; D earns $3.40 per hour and produces 127 units; and E earns $3.10 per hour and produces 89 units. Table 3.6 shows the calculation of gross wages.

As can be seen, the more an employee produces, the more he is paid at an ever-increasing bonus rate. This gives him the incentive to produce more because all units up to the changeover bonus percentage point are paid at the high rate. For example, D produced 127 units for a gross pay of $38.08. Had he produced only 124 units, his gross pay would have been $35.36 ($27.20 + [0.30 × $27.20]). Therefore, he earned an additional $2.72 by producing the extra three units.

The incentive plans discussed above are not the only ones, but they do give the reader an understanding of the rationale behind the company's wanting to devise a system for rewarding an employee's increased production in a given time space. Moreover, they are simple to understand and have been used successfully to secure increased efforts from employees.

Effect of Incentive Systems on Employers

Up to this point we have looked at incentive wage plans from the viewpoint of employee benefits. Is there a benefit for the employer?

Table 3.6

	Standard Production (1)	Actual Production (2)	Efficiency % (3) = (2) ÷ (1) × 100%	Percent Bonus Rate (4)	Actual Hours (5)	Wage Rate (6)	Hourly Gross Wages (7) = (5) × (6)	Final Gross Wages (8) = (7) + [(4) × (7)]
A	100	65	65	0%	8	$2.50	$20.00	$20.00
B	100	111	111	30	8	3.00	24.00	31.20
C	100	83	83	10	8	2.70	21.60	23.76
D	100	127	127	40	8	3.40	27.20	38.08
E	100	89	89	20	8	3.10	24.80	29.76

Table 3.7

	Units Produced (1)	Gross Wages (2)	Allocated Factory Overhead (3) = 8 × $10	Conversion Cost (4) = (2) + (3)	Conversion Cost/Unit (5) = (4) ÷ (1)
A	65	$20.00	$80.00	$100.00	$1.5385
C	83	23.76	80.00	103.76	1.2501
E	89	29.76	80.00	109.76	1.2333
B	111	31.20	80.00	111.20	1.0018
D	127	38.08	80.00	118.08	0.9298

There should be, and in the calculation of levels of incentive rates to pay, the employer is looking at an increased profit margin per unit to justify the increased labor cost of operation. This is the real measure for the employer because the unit price depends on costs, which include direct labor and allocated factory overhead.

Assuming factory overhead to be $10 per direct labor hour, and using the figures in Table 3.6 (the Emerson Efficiency Plan), we get the data in Table 3.7.

Thus, the reader can see that although employee D earned the most money (his objective), the company reduced its conversion cost per unit by 40 percent compared to A. This is substantial savings, and shows that by properly evaluating the costs of production, an incentive plan can be developed in many companies to aid in cutting per-unit cost by encouraging increased productivity. Reduced costs allow the company to be more competitive and enhance profitability.

PAYROLL TAXES PAID BY EMPLOYERS

Besides the gross wages earned by employees the employer must pay the appropriate government agency or insurance carrier an additional amount for social security and medicare, unemployment insurance, and workman's compensation.

The Social Security Act of 1935 established a plan for providing pensions at age 65 for employees then described in the Act. To finance this plan, the employee paid 1 percent of the first $3,000 earned and the employer paid an equal amount. This matching amount was an employer cost. Over the years, more and more persons have been covered under the Social Security system, and the rate of taxation and the amount of taxable wages has been periodically increased. Self-employed persons have also been covered. In 1976, amendments to the Act set a rate of 5.85 percent on the first $15,300 of wages earned, or a contribution of up to $895.05 by the employee and an equal amount by the employer.

Another federal-state tax on wages is for unemployment insurance. This tax was established by the Social Security Act of 1935. The Act acknowledged the responsibility of government to help the unemployed. This legislation delegated the job of setting up the employment services to the states, which were to collect the major portion of the tax to operate their own unemployment offices. State legislation had to conform to the requirements of the federal Act, and the employer could take a credit against the federal tax due for the amounts actually paid to the state system *or* for the maximum tax the state could levy on gross wages for unemployment tax purposes.

Built into the system was a merit-rating procedure to reward "good" employers (that is, employers who so operated their labor pool as to prevent repetitive hirings and firings and who fired employees only for good economic reasons). When a business was established (or entered the system), it paid the maximum state rate. If its employment record thereafter became stable, the rate dropped until the minimum rate was reached. Thus, the employer was rewarded in direct monetary terms for good employment practices.

At the present time all states (as well as Puerto Rico) are participating in this program. Alaska, Alabama, and New Jersey are the only states in which employees contribute to the fund; in all other states the tax is paid solely by employers. The Manpower Commission of the U.S. Department of Labor now acts as a coordinating body on the federal level. In 1975, the employer paid a maximum tax of 3.2 percent on wages up to $4,200 for each employee.

Workmen's compensation is a levy against employers for continuation of income to employees in periods when they cannot work because of accidents occurring on the job. The payments may be made to the state compensation insurance fund or to state-approved carriers. Employees are grouped into work types, and rates based on experience of risk incidence are established for each type. The cost of this insurance premium can be minimized by analyzing job contents properly and classifying employees in appropriate subgroups.

One of the problems faced by the payroll accounting department is the differing levels of gross wages for taxing purposes. Another is the identification of who is or is not an employer or an employee as defined by the various legislative acts.

The employer's cost of these benefits are charged to factory overhead or burden, and must ultimately end up in product cost.

OTHER FRINGE BENEFITS

Fringe benefits involve expenditures, other than payroll taxes and workmen's compensation insurance, that benefit employees individually or as a group. Since these are not legally required, they may vary from employer to employer and may be based on labor market competitiveness, industry practice, management's attitude toward employees, or management's social consciousness.

One such benefit is the portion of medical and dental insurance paid for by the employer. Medical insurance could cover the employee and his family for all or part of ordinary illness, or could apply only to catastrophic illnesses. Dental insurance might cover all or part of dental work needed by the worker and his family. Usually, a schedule of payments by the employee and the employer is established, a percentage of present employees are required to initiate the plan, and all new personnel are included automatically. The company's portion of the premium is the expense.

Another benefit is life insurance. Again a schedule is established, showing the employees' and employers' portion of the premium. In initiating this plan the personal histories of present employees are secured and a stated percentage of the work force must participate. All new personnel may be automatically included. The older the average age of the work force, the higher the premium per employee is generally. The company's portion of the premium is the expense.

Vacation pay is also considered a fringe benefit. Vacation policy varies from company to company as to length of the vacation. When the employee becomes eligible to participate, the amount of vacation earned but yet unpaid is a company liability, and this expense is an overhead charge.

Sick pay works similar to vacation pay. It may not be formally set up on the books as such, but is charged to overhead when taken. It can, however, be budgeted, based on past experience.

Another fringe benefit is an employee supplemental pension plan, which provides retirement benefits in addition to social security. It may be self-funded, in which case the company agrees to invest contributions required, or it may be funded by an outside agency such as an insurance company or a mutual fund company. In the latter case, the company makes the payments required under the plan. In a third arrangement, the plan may be fully funded by the company or partially by employees.

Under present Internal Revenue Code provisions, 15 percent of the employee's salary (up to $1,500) may be put into a pension plan, and income taxes on that amount will be deferred until the pension is activated. When an employee elects to defer the taxation on current income in this way, he must pay income taxes on the pension payments made in each calendar year when he starts to collect.

Because of the abuses in pension-plan administration in the past (such as retirees deprived of their pension because they were fired shortly before their retirement date; or ambiguous eligibility technicalities; or malfeasance in the administration of fund assets), Congress in recent years investigated the pension situation and took steps to correct these inequities. In 1974 it passed a pension reform law, known as ERISA (Employee Retirement Income Security Act), which established certain safeguards to protect the rights of employees.

Another fringe benefit is the stock-purchase plan, by which the company encourages employees to become shareholders in the company, allowing them to purchase stock at less than market value. The immediate benefit the employee receives is the difference between market price and the price he pays. The cost to the company may be at variance with that difference because market stock price is not the same as the value recorded in the company's books.

Other miscellaneous fringe-benefit expenses include:

1. Cost of operating the cafeteria, less receipts for sales made. The benefit to the employee is the difference between what he would pay for the food and beverage in an outside cafeteria and what he pays at the plant.
2. Cost of equipping and operating the in-plant medical facilities.
3. Cost of purchasing, paving, and maintaining the employee parking lot.
4. Cost of equipping and operating sports teams and leagues, funding and supervising Christmas bonuses, and maintaining incidental employee conveniences.

One must not lose sight of the fact that the employer's cost must be passed on to the consumer ultimately. In a study made by the Chamber of Commerce of the United States, it was found that nationwide fringe benefits run to 32.7 percent of gross wages!

DIRECT LABOR DISTRIBUTION

It is important to remember that the direct labor charge to production is what is earned in making the product. So that management will have means of controlling direct and indirect costs, it should not relate the charge for gross wages to the employee, but should relate it to what the employee does. While the employee is physically engaged in making the product, the gross wages earned (with some exceptions) should be charged to production. When he is shifted to a nongoods-producing job, his gross wages earned should be charged to an appropriate overhead account. If the employee is standing by while his machine is being repaired, the charge should be to "Factory

Overhead—Machine Breakdown," and the account charges should be analyzed to prevent future breakdown as far as possible. If the employee is standing by while waiting for parts because of improper scheduling, the charge should be to "Factory Overhead—Scheduling Delays," and the account charges should be analyzed to correct the poor scheduling procedures. In this way management can pinpoint the responsibilities for direct labor costs that produce no goods and can thus lay the foundation for a good responsibility accounting structure.

When possible, the production employee should be transferred to an indirect labor job when he cannot work on production. He may be transferred to the stockroom to replenish stock shelves or to the internal transportation department to assist in moving goods that create a bottleneck in the production process, and thus help to smooth out production flow. Where a union contract prevents this sort of shift, it is incumbent on management to strive to reduce this lost time by using production workers as much as possible in production.

One question that arises is the charge for bonuses paid to production workers for excess production. This may be handled by charging to production the gross wages earned, or by splitting the gross wages into hours worked times rate per hour and charging that to production, and charging the remainder of the gross wages to a bonus account. In either case, the total gross wages will ultimately be included in costs of production.

INDIRECT LABOR DISTRIBUTION

All factory gross wages other than those used in production of goods are chargeable to factory overhead. Thus, the salaries of the manufacturing manager, factory purchasing agent, factory accountant, factory quality control supervisor, factory receiving foreman, etc., and of the personnel in their immediate departments are included. For purposes of responsibility accounting these various salaries might well be collected by department or by functional area so that the responsible party can watch these costs and control them. This will assist the responsible party in preparing budgets of costs for subsequent periods.

Included in factory overhead are vacation pay, sick pay, and other paid leaves granted to production workers. Also, as pointed out above, the bonuses paid for excess production might appear here if the accounting system so segregates those charges.

Use of the Computer in Payroll Computations and Distribution

One of the early business uses of the computer was in payroll accounting. The program could be written to include the appropriate federal withholding tables (now also state and/or city taxes), FICA tax rate and limits, disability insurance rate and limits, and other appropriate data for deductions (the employee's name, pay rate, withholding status). Then, given the employee's name and current pay-period data, the computer would compute gross wages on the bases of both time and work performance, and then prepare a payroll showing the proper gross wages, all deductions, and net pay. If the input of data was also coded by job or process number, or by appropriate department, it could analyze and report a summary of gross wages by job or process number and by corresponding departments.

Today, with banks and service bureaus ready to perform these functions for business, a relatively small manufacturer can avail itself of this type of data processing. These services also prepare year-to-date totals for each employee, prepare required quarterly and yearly payroll tax reports, make proper payments to the governmental agency for amounts withheld and the employer's portion of tax due, prepare a yearly individual employee's earnings record and the W-2 forms needed for yearly income reports to the federal government. The W-2 reports to the government are necessary for the purpose of recapping social security and withholding taxes by employee. The employee needs a copy to file with his federal income tax return and state and city income tax returns (if required). The employer retains a copy for his record.

QUESTIONS

1. Discuss the relative benefits to production workers of time-attendance computation of gross wages and incentive computation.

2. Why is it better to have an Emerson Efficiency Plan than a straight piecework plan?

3. (a) What are the employee deductions required by law, and (b) how do they affect costs?

4. (a) What are the employer payroll taxes required by law, and (b) how do they affect costs?

5. (a) Why are fringe benefits given to employees, and (b) what is the justification for them?

6. Under an incentive plan, the following table shows the results of payroll computation. Would you conclude that this is a good plan?

	Units Produced	Gross Wages	Allocated Factory Overhead	Conversion Cost
A	66	$45.80	$40.00	$ 85.80
B	128	88.00	40.00	128.00
C	73	51.25	40.00	91.25
D	115	69.25	40.00	109.25
E	87	38.30	40.00	78.30

4

Raw Materials Management

RAW materials represent a large investment in a company. The science of inventory management is one that has been developing rapidly over the past decade, and proper inventory management can save the company much money. Raw materials are purchased, processed, and stored prior to being put into production, and are readily identifiable in the accounting records. But there is much inventory in process where the partly completed product is the link between production processes. This is not readily perceivable in the accounting records because materials are merged with labor and overhead in the Work-in-Process account. Therefore, inventory management must have knowledge of inventory movement in and out of stores, average inventory, safety stock, lead time, and reorder points. It must understand the purchasing procedures, and must balance purchase and holding costs to achieve the lowest per-unit cost of purchase at time of use. It must know what quantity to order so as to achieve this minimization of cost. Chapter 5 deals with accounting methods and alternative procedures for controlling these data.

INVENTORY MANAGEMENT

Raw materials enter the plant after the purchasing agent places an order, the materials are received, and the storeroom checks them in. The storeroom must make them readily available for distribution to the production process as needed. When a production order is issued, the storekeeper should get a document relieving him of responsibility for the goods released and this document should transfer the responsibility for use of the goods to someone else. The order signed by the recipient becomes the basis for charging the goods to the proper production account. An example of this document, sometimes called the "Storeroom Requisition," is shown in Figure 4.1.

Figure 4.1

| STOREROOM REQUISITION | | | Req. No. _____ |

Storekeeper: Please furnish bearer with the following.   Date_____19___

Charge Acct. No._____ Dept._____Dept. No._____

QUANTITY	ARTICLES	STOCK NO.	PRICE	AMOUNT

CHARGE JOB NO.	ENTERED ON STOCK LEDGER	ENTERED ON RECAP.	Signed

PRINTED IN U.S.A.   STORE-ROOM REQUISITION

The person needing the material presents it to the storekeeper, showing what is wanted by part number and quantity, what job or process it is to be used in, and the proper authorizing signatures. The storekeeper has the responsibility of having goods on hand when they are required. Therefore he must keep track of inventory movement and anticipate demand by ordering sufficiently in advance of requests so that material will be on hand as needed. Yet he must not have an excess of material on hand so that the inventory investment becomes a burden on the finances of the company. Ideally, there should be no inventory. Practically, however, we cannot expect instantaneous delivery of material by the supplier when we need it. Therefore the company must anticipate its needs and minimize its costs of inventory.

A simple diagram may help to show the way working capital can be tied up in inventory as a result of improper management. Assume that the company uses 20 units of item A per workday and decides to order a 30-day supply every 30 workdays. The company assumes a lead time (time from the issuance of a purchase order to date of delivery) of 15 workdays. Figure 4.2 is a graph of these data (on a 15-day lead time), where A is the reorder point for 300 units. The average inventory investment is $((600 - 0)/2) \times \$10$, or $3,000.

If the lead time is shown to be incorrect by making a study of actual lead time (5 days) as reflected in delivered orders, then a graph of the inventory would look like Figure 4.3, where A indicates the reorder point of 300 units. The average inventory after 20 days is $200 + [(800 - 200)/2]$ or 500 units. If the units each cost $10, this is an average investment of $5,000. This is an increase in average inventory over that planned of $2,000. At 10 percent annual rate of return, this error would decrease profits by $200 on this item alone.

If the purchasing agent changes the procedure to order five days before the item runs out (100 units of inventory), then a graph of the inventory would look like Figure 4.4. Now the average inventory is $[(600 - 0)/2]$, or 300 units at $10 per unit, as originally planned.

However, in this example, if there were a longer lead time (say, 30 workdays), there might be a danger that material needed would not be available (that is, a stock-out). This would also be a possibility if there were a dramatic increase in the demand for production units.

If the item is a standard item locally available, and the five-day lead time is rarely exceeded, it might be advisable to continue with the new purchase policy; that is, risk an occasional stock-out and have the lower inventory investment, thereby saving the $200 on this item each year. However, if the part is a special part not locally available, the company might want to insure against a stock-out by having a small reserve stock of, say, 10 percent of the entire 30-workday supply (600 units). A graph of the inventory movement would look like Figure 4.5, where A indicates the reorder point as 160 units (on the basis of a five-day lead time plus safety stock).

Counting the safety stock, the average inventory would be 60

Figure 4.2 Original purchase plan.

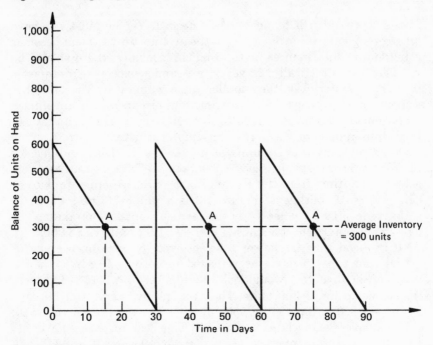

Figure 4.3 Original purchase plan effects due to lead-time error.

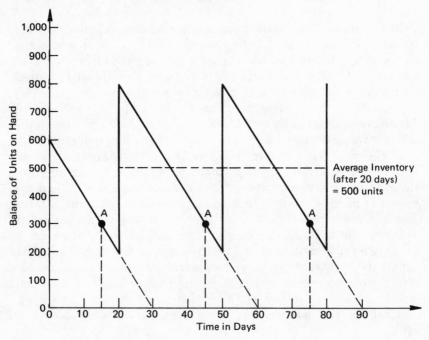

Figure 4.4   Modified purchase plan.

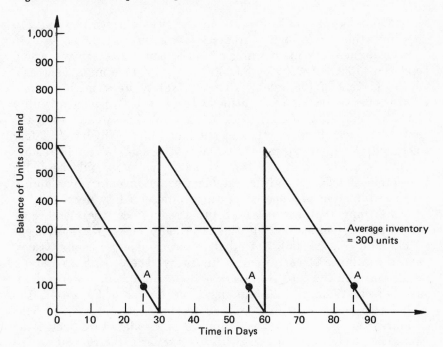

Figure 4.5   Modified purchase plan with safety stock.

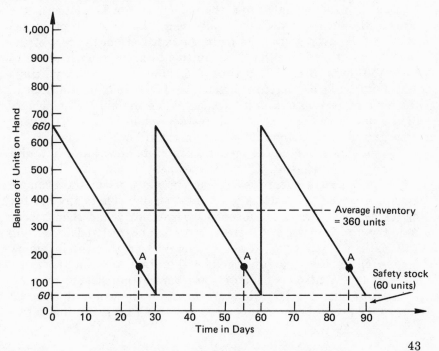

+ [(660 − 60)/2], or 360 units on the fifteenth workday; at $10 per unit, this would be an inventory investment of $3,600. At a 10 percent annual rate, maintaining a reserve to prevent stock-outs would cost $60 [10% × ($3,600 − $3,000)] per year. One might now ask, "Is 10 percent of the order realistic for safety stock on this item?" The answer would have to be made in terms of ready part availability and the possibility of having an actual lead time greater than the anticipated lead time. Another question might be, "Why have a safety stock margin equal to three additional days' usage?" As can be readily seen, a study of lead times from various suppliers should be made, exceptions noted, probabilities established, and inventory availability reviewed in order to properly set the amount of safety stock.

One thing that has not been discussed is how the storekeeper reorders the item at the right time. Normally, the storekeeper keeps a bin card (Figure 4.6). Note that this card shows receipts, issues, and the balance of each item in inventory. There is also a reorder point noted on the card [in Figure 4.4 it would be 100 units without safety stock (5 days × 20 units used per day) or in Figure 4.5 160 units with safety stock (5 days × 20 units used per day) + 60]. This requires the storekeeper to calculate a new balance on each issue and compare the new balance with the reorder point. Should he fail to do this, or should the card balance be above the actual balance because of an arithmetic error, the order may not be placed at the scheduled time and a stock-out could occur. This might be prevented by physically segregating the reorder quantity from the rest of the inventory at time of receipt. If, as in this case, the reorder quantity were 100 units (5 days lead time × 20 units used per day), these 100 units could be stored in a separate bin or put in the back of the bin wrapped up in a unit package. When the bin became empty or the unit package was reached, reorder would be more positively assured and stock-outs would be minimized, if not eliminated.

Let us now examine changes in usage rate downward, but with no change in purchasing policy. The company would order 600 units (600 = 30-workday supply) every 30 workdays, as in the example before. However, usage drops to 15 units per day, due to any number of reasons. The graph for inventory movement would then appear as in Figure 4.7, in which A represents the balance on hand (increasing with each new purchase). It can be readily seen that the inventory is growing in size, by an average of 150 units (600 − 450) for every 30 workdays. Therefore, a purely mechanical purchasing plan for a part can absorb a large increase in inventory value. It is hoped that no company buys on this basis and that this is an illustration

Figure 4.6   Bin card.

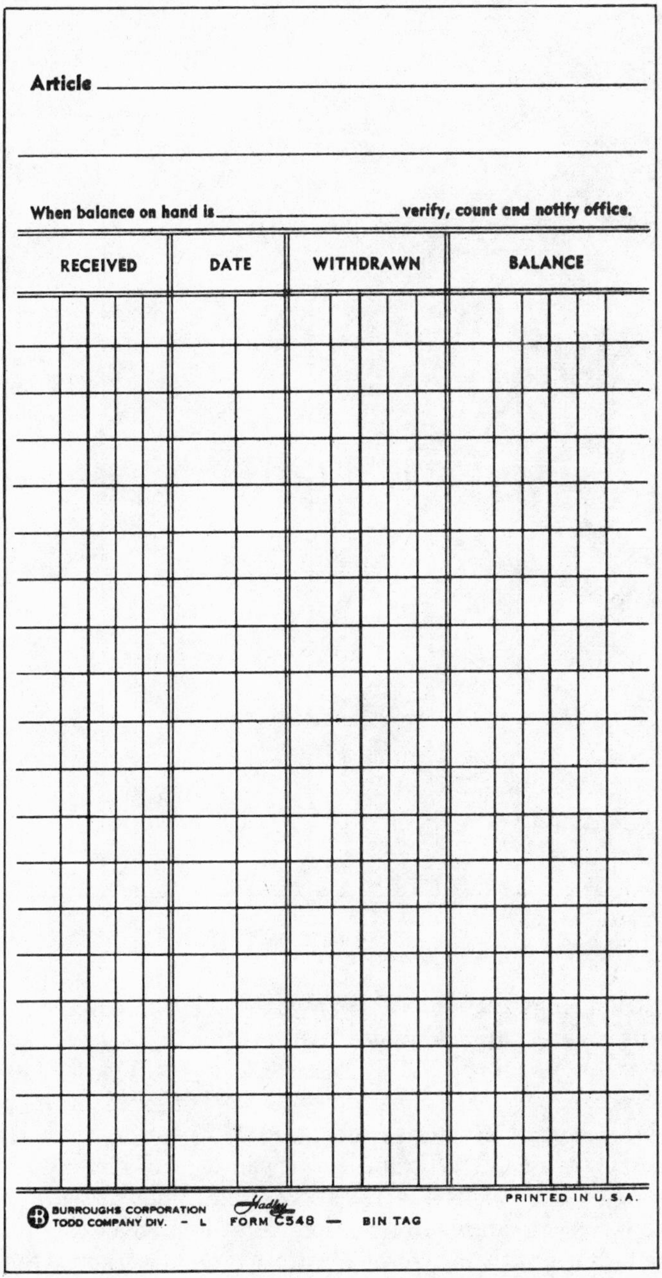

Article _____

_____

When balance on hand is _____ verify, count and notify office.

RECEIVED	DATE	WITHDRAWN	BALANCE

BURROUGHS CORPORATION
TODD COMPANY DIV. - L   FORM C548 — BIN TAG   PRINTED IN U.S.A.

Figure 4.7   Original purchase plan with decreased usage.

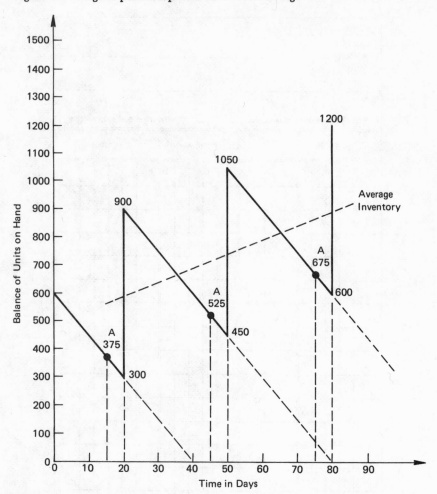

only of what *might* possibly happen with such a purchasing policy.

Let us now examine changes in the usage rate upward, with no change in purchasing policy. The company will order 600 units (30-workday supply) over a period of 30 workdays, as in the previous example. However, usage has increased to 25 units per day, for any number of reasons. The graph for inventory movement looks like Figure 4.8, where A is the reorder point and S indicates the stock-out condition. Here it can readily be seen that the increased usage causes stock-outs at the 48th day, 74th day, and every 30 workdays thereafter.

Figure 4.8 Original purchase plan with increased usage.

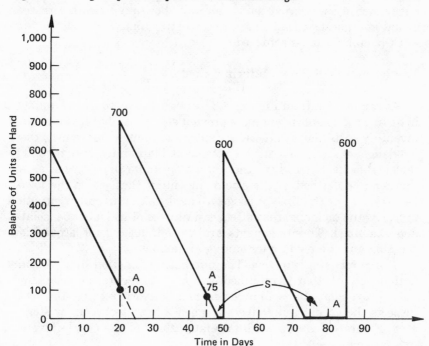

This requires special activity, spot purchases, etc., or the employment of safety stock in order to keep the operation going.

COMPUTER USAGE FOR DATA

Figures 4.2 through 4.8 show clearly that the purchasing and inventory control functions must be mated on more than a purely time basis or prior analysis basis. The person in charge of each function must have certain information that the person in charge of the other function knows so that both can do their job better and prevent excessive cost of (1) excessive safety stock provisions or (2) frequent stock-outs.

The utility of a computer in these two functional areas can be readily seen. If the inventory data are put in the computer and receipts are promptly posted and stock issuances promptly processed, the computer can generate daily usage reports, a comparison of actual and planned daily usage, and a daily inventory balance. When properly programmed, the computer can prepare a report showing which items have reached the reorder point, and can show any variance between actual and planned lead time so that better control of ordering and stock balances can be achieved.

The Elements of Raw Materials Cost

As can be seen from Figures 4.2 through 4.8, there are advantages in having sufficient inventory to prevent stock-outs, but this increased inventory costs money. If the inventory is reduced too much, there is a danger of stock-outs and the attendant additional cost in inventory replenishment. Somewhere there is an optimum inventory size, and this may be defined as the size of inventory that yields the lowest per-unit cost at the time of usage. To analyze the inventory situation properly, the elements that affect cost at time of use must be isolated and examined. These elements are the purchasing (or acquisition) function and the holding (or storage) functions.

The purchasing function. The purchasing function in a company is that activity that is informed of a need to secure material, finds the right vendor, places an order, insures delivery, receives the goods, inspects the goods, and delivers the goods to a stockroom or storage area. Figure 4.9 shows the interrelationships of the people involved in a purchase.

The trigger for a purchase is the Purchase Requisition prepared by the storekeeper, who checks the balance of the bin card against the reorder quantity shown on the bin card, or who must draw on the segregated minimum quantity to fill a production requisition, or by a computer that checks the minimum quantity against the balance on hand after issuance of material.

The purchasing agent then determines who the vendor will be after reviewing specifications, delivery dates, quantity, price, and terms. He may request bids or may place the order directly. His notification to the vendor is a Purchase Order. Copies of the Purchase Order are distributed to the issuer of the Purchase Requisition, to notify him that the purchase has been initiated; to the receiving department, so it can anticipate the work load of materials receipts (this may not show quantity ordered so that a physical count of incoming goods will verify order fulfillment, but may show cubic volume of the purchase to insure enough space to receive it); to the inspection department to alert it of inspection requirements (if any); and to the accounting department so that it can budget cash require-

Figure 4.9 Interrelationships of purchasing functions.

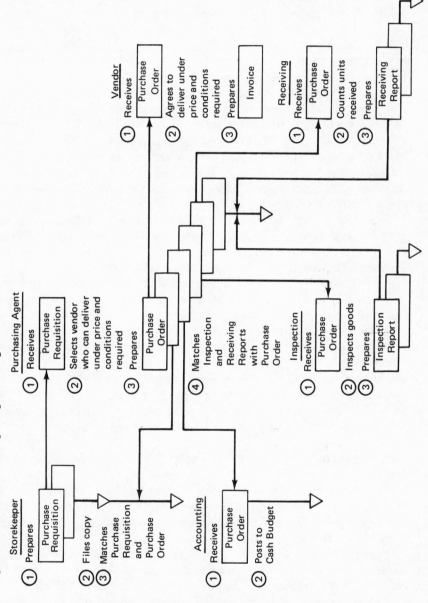

ments. The purchasing department keeps a copy for follow-up and expediting purposes.

The vendor, having received the order, accepts it by formal acknowledgment and/or by shipping the goods requested. These are delivered to the receiving department where the items are counted and a Receiving Report is sent to the purchasing department to acknowledge receipt. The purchasing agent compares the quantity received with the order; if there is a shortage the vendor is contacted to insure completion of the order. If there is to be an inspection, the goods or a sample are delivered to the inspection department to verify usability of the material and to prepare an Inspection Report. This report is sent to the purchasing department, which accepts or rejects the goods. If accepted, the goods go to the storeroom or warehouse; if rejected, the purchasing agent notifies the vendor and negotiates with him for replacement, adjustment, etc., and the goods are accepted or returned.

The cost of the purchasing function includes, then, the cost of staffing and operating the purchasing department, the receiving department, the inspection department, the group that prepares the Purchase Requisition, and the group in the accounting department that budgets cash requirements. These costs include salaries of personnel plus fringe benefits related thereto, telephone, office supplies, utilities, depreciation on office and other equipment, taxes and insurance on personal property, etc. Where the space and personnel are used for both receiving and shipping, costs must be made prorated; where space and personnel are used for both inspection of incoming goods and inspection of production, a prorating must also be done.

All these costs together are the purchasing costs, and may have to be summarized from various general ledger accounts. Later in this chapter, the costs will be referred to when economic lot quantity is discussed.

The holding function. Once accepted, the goods are delivered to the storeroom or warehouse for storage until needed in production. During the period of time between placing the goods in storage and issuing them to production, the goods must be segregated by type for easy accessibility and must be protected from damage, destruction, fire, and theft.

One question that must be answered is whether the company should have centralized or decentralized storerooms. The arguments for centralized storerooms are that they provide (1) more efficient use of stores personnel, allowing specialization within the group; (2) better security against theft and fire; and (3) more efficient use of space and handling equipment. The arguments for decentralized storerooms are that they insure (1) more efficient use of production personnel, who do not have to travel so far for stores; and (2) more efficient design of particular storerooms. Which is better can be answered only by a study of the individual plant. It is important to collect data on storage patterns, movement patterns, size of inventory, etc., to determine a system that increases efficiency in the storage function, and it is important to review those data inputs on a periodic basis or when plant conditions change.

Security is an important consideration today because of the feeling that small amounts of material won't be missed, that business is "bad" so it is "just" to take from it, and that pilfering is so common no one will notice or even think it is wrong. The distinction today between moral right and wrong, and other ethical considerations, is considerably blurred. It is interesting to note that the Bureau of Domestic Commerce (U.S. Department of Commerce) estimates $20.3 billion as the cost of crimes against business in America in 1974. This amounts to 1.5 percent of the Gross National Product, although the total cost is unknown and may be many times higher. The problem of security includes the intrusion into the company of those who harbor ill will toward the company (for whatever reasons) and want to destroy by arson or explosion the physical assets of the company. Anyone traveling by air knows of increased security at airports, and everyone associated with industry knows that the private detection business in plant security has expanded tremendously in the past decade.

The costs of the holding function include, then, the cost of staffing and operating the storerooms and warehouses where raw materials are kept as well as the cost of staffing and operating security systems to prevent loss from damage, fire, and theft. These costs include salaries of personnel plus fringe benefits, telephone, office and other supplies, utilities, depreciation on equipment, taxes and insurance on the raw materials and equipment, etc. Where the space and personnel are used for both storage and handling of raw materials and finished goods, prorating of costs must be done; where the security system is used for raw materials, production, finished goods, and other security, prorating is also necessary. Other costs, not mentioned above, will be deterioration and obsolescence of the goods, interest on average inventory, and depreciation of storage facilities.

All these costs are together the holding costs and may have to be summarized from various general ledger accounts. These will be discussed with the purchasing costs to determine the economic order quantity.

Economic Order Quantity

In previous discussions no mention has been made of a generalized formula for determining reorder quantity. The examples used earlier in this chapter were based on a 30-workday supply. Any arbitrary figure could have been selected for the amount of items required. The question that must be answered is, "In view of purchasing and storage costs what size order is best?" Studies have been made of this problem, and formulas have been developed to assist in estimating an economic order quantity.

Table 4.1

Units Ordered (1)	Ordering Cost/Unit (2) = \$75 ÷ (1)
100	\$0.7500
200	0.3750
300	0.2500
400	0.1875
500	0.1500
600	0.1250
700	0.1071
800	0.0938
900	0.0833
1,000	0.0750

Table 4.2

Units Purchased (1)	Average Inventory (Units) (2) = (1) ÷ 2	Average Inventory (3) = (2) × \$20	Total Holding Costs (4) = (3) × 5%	Holding Cost/ Unit (6) = (4) ÷ 2,000
100	50	\$ 1,000	\$ 50	0.0250
200	100	2,000	100	0.0500
300	150	3,000	150	0.0750
400	200	4,000	200	0.1000
500	250	5,000	250	0.1250
600	300	6,000	300	0.1500
700	350	7,000	350	0.1750
800	400	8,000	400	0.2000
900	450	9,000	450	0.2250
1,000	500	10,000	500	0.2500

To illustrate the development of this technique, a model is adopted here. The total purchasing cost per year is $750,000, and 10,000 orders are processed. The total holding cost is $40,000, and the average inventory is $800,000. The quantity used per year is 2,000 units. The cost per unit is $20. The cost to process an order is $75.

$$\$750,000 \div 10,000 \text{ orders} = \$75 \text{ per order}$$

The more units purchased in one purchase order, the lower the purchasing cost per unit. Table 4.1 lists the varying costs of different quantities ordered at a basic price of $75 per order.

The cost of holding a unit can be determined by taking the value

Figure 4.10 Economic order quantity chart.

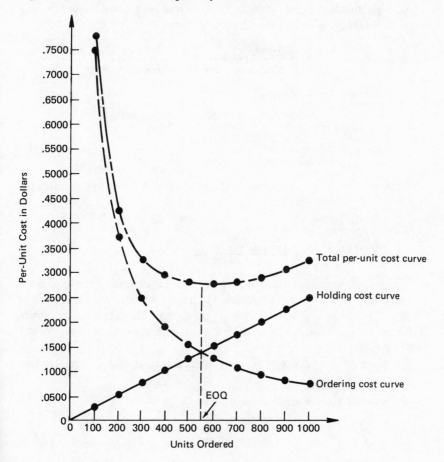

of the average inventory and multiplying it by the holding factor expressed as a percentage of average inventory. In our example, the data generate a holding cost of 5 percent:

$$\$40,000 \div \$800,000 \times 100\% = 5\%$$

Table 4.2 shows the cost per unit of varying amounts purchased. Figure 4.10 combines the data of Tables 4.1 and 4.2 on one chart. It can be seen that as the number of units in the purchase go up, the *purchase cost per unit goes down,* but the *holding cost per unit goes up.* When the two curves are added together, the total per-unit cost curve is developed; this curve will dip as far down as 550 or so, and then turn upward. The point where the two basic curves cross is called the "economic order quantity" (EOQ).

Since application of this technique is very laborious and costly, some other method must be devised. This has been done by developing various formulas to generate the EOQ. Once such formula is

$$EOQ = \sqrt{\frac{2 \times (\text{purchase cost/order}) \times (\text{usage in units/year})}{(\text{invoice cost/unit}) \times (\text{holding cost})^*}}$$

Substituting the data given, the computation is

$$EOQ = \sqrt{\frac{2 \times \$75 \times 2,000}{\$20 \times 5\%}} = \sqrt{\frac{300,000}{1}}$$

$$= 547 \text{ approx.}$$

The use of a formula simplifies the computation process and eliminates the need for tables and graphs of the data

ADDITIONAL COMPUTER USAGE FOR DATA

If the computer data described earlier in this chapter were expanded to include price and the program expanded to include instructions to develop usage for the preceding year and the steps to compute *EOQ*, it could present the *EOQ* for all items that have reached the reorder point.

Further data and programming instruction might be inserted so

---

*expressed as a percentage of average inventory:

$$\frac{\text{holding costs (\$)}}{\text{average inventory}} \times 100\%$$

that purchase orders could be prepared by the computer and addressed to the proper vendors. Then these orders need be reviewed only for appropriateness by the purchasing agent before mailing or delivering to vendors.

QUESTIONS

1. Assume no safety stock. If the usage is 52 units per day and the lead time is calculated at seven working days, what is the reorder point?

2. Assume an average inventory of $250,000, which includes safety stock of $30,000. An analysis of safety stock requirements is made and the new safety stock is shown to be $10,000. How much is saved annually at a 10 percent rate of return?

Figure 4.11 Question 3.

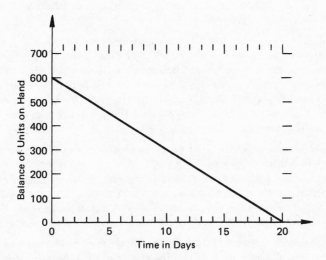

3. The usage rate for item A is 30 units per day and enough is ordered for 20 workdays. The lead time is 5 days. On Figure 4.11 indicate the day for reorder and the reorder size point.

4. The usage rate has been 25 units per day, with an order of 700 units and a lead time of 6 days. The usage rate has changed to 35 units per day, but no change has been made in the reorder point. On Figure 4.12,

Figure 4.12   Question 4.

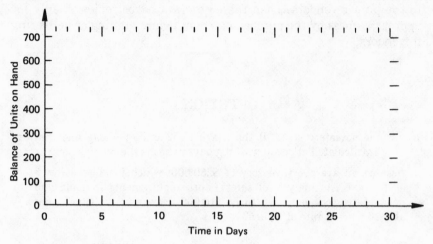

show the old usage rate, the new usage rate, and the number of days there will be a stock-out (assume no emergency purchases and no safety stock). This may be tricky!

5. A study of all purchase costs in the past year reveals that salaries amount to $200,000 and fringe benefits to $60,000; other costs are $140,000. Four thousand purchase orders were processed. It is expected that salaries in the present year will increase 5 percent; fringe benefits, 7 percent; and other costs, 8 percent. It is also estimated that 4,500 purchase orders will be processed. What are the old and the projected purchase cost per order (to the nearest dollar)?

6. A study showed that all holding costs in the past year were $400,000 and average inventory was $1,200,000. A projection of cost for this year shows holding costs will increase 30 percent. A review of safety stock shows that inventory can be decreased 25 percent, but that replacement costs will average a 10 percent increase in the following year. What are the old and the projected holding costs, expressed as a percentage?

7. Using the correct answers for Questions 5 and 6 (see answers), and assuming item A has a usage of 1,200 units per year at a per-unit cost of $25 last year and $35 this year, compute the EOQ for both years.

5

Raw Materials—
Accounting Concepts

THE accountant is interested in inventory management (and frequently advises on procedures to improve it), but his primary concern is record keeping. He is interested in how much material went into production and in the cost of that material. The accounting profession has developed two methods to ascertain inventory usage and the remaining inventory. These are the periodic and the perpetual inventory systems. The better of these two systems, from the standpoint of production management, is the perpetual inventory system.

The accountant is also interested in the price of the units charged to production and left in inventory. The earliest pricing system used followed the movement of the goods; this is called first-in–first-out (FIFO), and is an excellent system if price levels are fairly constant. The average and moving-average methods were developed to smooth out small increases in price level or seasonal price differences. In the World War II era, when price levels started to increase more rapidly, the last-in–first-out (LIFO) system was devised to present a fairer income statement. Each of these methods affects the value of ending inventory and the value of the materials placed into production. The Internal Revenue Code recognizes both FIFO and LIFO, and company management may select whichever method is most advantageous and will present the fairest income. However, once a method is chosen, it cannot be changed without the express permission of the local director of the Internal Revenue Service.

INVENTORY SYSTEMS

The Periodic Inventory System

In using the periodic inventory system, the accountant sets up two accounts: an asset account, called Raw Materials, which reflects the value of the inventory at the first day of the year; and an expense account, called Purchases, which reflects the purchase of all raw materials during the fiscal period, less purchase returns and allowances. At the end of the fiscal period he counts the remaining inventory, prices it out, and determines the amount of materials used by the formula

Beginning inventory + net purchases − ending inventory
= materials used

The accountant usually presents this in tabular form as

	Beginning raw materials inventory	$XX
(+)	Purchases during period (net)	XX
		XX
(−)	Less: Ending raw materials inventory	XX
(=)	Materials used	$XX

During the fiscal period the actual amount of units of an item is not part of the accounting records (there may be bin cards) and so is not known. At the end of the year the plant must be closed for taking inventory, or if it is kept open, the operations must be controlled so they do not interfere with the inventory process.

In smaller companies where the risk of loss from theft is small, or where the dollar value per space volume is relatively low, or where the inventory is not large, or where the plant can economically be closed down, this end-of-year method may be practical. It requires little record keeping in addition to that necessary to record the purchases, but it gives less ongoing control over inventory than might be desired.

The Perpetual Inventory System

The perpetual inventory system differs from the periodic system in that it is constantly updated. In addition to bin cards being kept at the storeroom, a set of inventory cards (developed from source data) is kept in the accounting department. The accounting department can check the count at any time during the year, not just at year's end, and can start investigating any irregularities found. The production department can ask the accounting department about balances and can rely more on accounting figures because the accounting department acts only in its accounting role, not a custodial role (which might be inclined to feed erroneous data into the system to cover up unexplained discrepancies). The accountant uses only one account, the Raw Materials Inventory, which represents the dollar value of inventory at the beginning of the period *and* the purchases of inventory during the period (net) *less* the value of the inventory used in production.

The value of the inventory used in production is determined by requiring all goods taken out of stores to be signed for by the recipient, who specifies the job or process number the material is to be used on, and the items desired and their quantities. The withdrawal document is sometimes called a Storeroom Requisition and is sent to the accounting department where it is priced out (according to the pricing system in use at the plant), is summarized, and becomes the basis for accounting entries that reduce Raw Materials Inventory and increase Work-in-Process Inventory.

The perpetual inventory system is more expensive to maintain than the periodic inventory system because it requires setting up and posting to a set of inventory cards in the accounting department in addition to the bin cards. However, when it is used, the accounting department can make a physical count more often than once a year because the inventory cards can be checked at any time against the physical count. The company hopes to more than offset this additional cost by savings realized through better inventory control.

The system also contains data that can be studied and used for timely inventory ordering, economic order-size computation, usage trend analysis, safety stock requirements analysis, and lead-time computation.

PRICING SYSTEMS

Whenever units of inventory are transferred from the storeroom to production, the value of those items must be ascertained by some rationale if the unit cost of the items purchased should vary. Four major pricing methods are now discussed.

First-In–First-Out (FIFO) Pricing System

From a usage standpoint it makes sense to use the physically oldest material on hand before using the material just received. It was an easy extension of this concept to use the oldest prices first, leaving the newest prices in inventory. In periods where prices tended to fluctuate slightly above and slightly below a gradually rising price-trend line, this pricing system gave good results from the accountant's viewpoint because the balance sheet was fairly stated (which was the auditor's primary interest and where the major audit emphasis was made). The costs were derived by rearrangement of the formula stated earlier: materials used = beginning inventory + purchases (net) − ending inventory.

An example will illustrate the pricing under LIFO. Analysis of inventory movement is shown in Table 5.1. The first 40 units used are at $6.00 each leaving 60 at $6.00 each. The next 65 used are 60 at $6.00 each and 5 at $6.05 each (the January 1 balance on hand is completely used up, 5 of the February 14 purchase at $6.05 each are used, and the balance of 45 left in inventory are at $6.05 each). The next 55 used are 45 at $6.05 each and 10 at $6.02 each (the balance of the February 14 purchase at $6.05 is completely used up, 10 of the March 10 purchase at $6.02 are used, and the balance is 50 units at $6.02 each). Under the periodic inventory method, the usage might be shown as in Table 5.2. Under the perpetual inventory

Table 5.1

		In	Out	Balance
Jan. 1	Balance on hand @ $6.00			100
Jan. 31	Usage		40	60
Feb. 14	Purchase @ $6.05	50		110
Feb. 28	Usage		65	45
Mar. 10	Purchase @ $6.02	60		105
Mar. 31	Usage		55	50

Table 5.2

	Beginning Inventory:	100 @ $6.00	$ 600.00
(+)	Purchases:	50 @ $6.05	302.50
		60 @ $6.02	361.20
			$1,263.70
(−)	Ending Inventory:	50 @ $6.02	301.00
	Materials used		$ 962.70

Table 5.3

		In	Out	Balance
Jan. 1	Balance on hand @ $6.00			100 – $6.00
Jan. 31	Usage, 40		40	60 – $6.00
				60 – $6.00
Feb. 14	Purchase @ $6.05	50		50 – $6.05
Feb. 28	Usage, 65		65	45 – $6.05
Mar. 10	Purchase @ $6.02	60		45 – $6.05
				60 – $6.02
Mar. 31	Usage, 55		55	50 – $6.02
Total		110	160	

Table 5.4

Jan. 31	Usage	40 @ $6.00		$240.00
Feb. 28	Usage, 65	60 @ $6.00	$360.00	
		5 @ $6.05	30.25	390.25
Mar. 31	Usage, 55	45 @ $6.05	$272.25	
		10 @ $6.02	60.20	332.45
	Materials used			$962.70

system, the record card for this item would be expanded for each in price selection, and might look like Table 5.3. The amount to be charged to Work-in-Process Inventory would be developed as in Table 5.4. The ending inventory would be $301.00 (50 at $6.02 each).

As can be seen, neither the periodic nor the perpetual inventory system changes the material used, nor does it change the ending

inventory prices reached by using the FIFO pricing method. Note
that the ending inventory consists of the latest prices.

Average Pricing System

This pricing system is suitable for use with the periodic system.
A record (Table 5.5) is kept of the beginning inventory and all purchases
(using data shown in Table 5.1). Thus, the tabulation shows the total
(210) of all units available for use, the total cost ($1,263.70) of those
units, and the average unit cost ($6.018). Then the ending inventory
is counted and priced (50 units at $6.018), and the difference is assumed
to have been used in production.

Moving-Average Pricing System

With this pricing system a new average is developed after each
purchase (the units at the time of the receipt are added to inventory
value). This system is applicable when the perpetual inventory system
is used. Taking data from Table 5.1, the prices are recorded as shown
in Table 5.6. The balance of inventory is computed as the goods are
issued and entered into the records.

Last-In–First-Out (LIFO) Pricing System

Under this pricing system, goods still physically move on a first-in–
first-out basis, but the pricing is restructured to a last-in–first-out
basis. The latest (newest) prices are charged to production and the
oldest prices are left in inventory. The rationale behind LIFO is that
in periods of advancing prices the replacement cost of goods used
is closer to the latest prices paid than to the oldest prices paid, and
that these later costs will more accurately match current income and
current expense. The figures in Table 5.1 are again used in Table

Table 5.5

Beginning Inventory	100 @ $6.00	$ 600.00
Purchase Feb. 14	50 @ $6.05	302.50
Purchase Mar. 10	60 @ $6.02	361.20
Averaging	210 @ $6.018	$1,263.70
Inventory	50 @ $6.018	300.90
Used in Production	160 @ $6.018	$ 962.80 (rounded)

Table 5.6

Date	Description	In Units	In Amount	Out Units	Out Amount	Balance Units	Balance Unit Cost	Balance Amount
Jan. 1	Balance on hand					100	$6.000	$600.00
Jan. 31	Usage			40	$240.00	60		360.00
Feb. 14	Purchase	50	$302.50			110	$6.023	662.50
Feb. 28	Usage			65	391.50	45		271.00
Mar. 10	Purchase	60	361.20			105	$6.021	632.20
Mar. 31	Usage			55	331.16	50		301.04
		110	$663.70	160	$962.66			

Table 5.7

Date	Description	In Units	In Amount	Out Units	Out Amount	Balance Units	Balance Unit Cost	Balance Amount
Jan. 1	Balance on hand					100	$6.000	$600.00
Jan. 31	Usage			40	$240.00	60	6.000	360.00
Feb. 14	Purchase	50	$302.50			60	6.000	360.00
						50	6.050	302.50
Feb. 28	Usage			50	302.50	45	6.000	270.00
				15	90.00			
Mar. 10	Purchase	60	361.20			45	6.000	270.00
						60	6.020	361.20
Mar. 28	Usage			55	331.10	45	6.000	270.00
						5	6.020	30.10
		110	$663.70	160	$963.60			$300.10

Table 5.8

	FIFO		Average		Moving Average		LIFO	
	Units	Amount	Units	Amount	Units	Amount	Units	Amount
Beginning Inventory	100	$ 600.00	100	$ 600.00	100	$ 600.00	100	$ 600.00
Purchases	110	663.70	110	663.70	110	663.70	110	663.70
Goods available	210	$1,263.70	210	$1,263.70	210	$1,263.70	210	$1,263.70
Materials used	160	$ 962.70	160	$ 962.80	160	$ 962.66	160	$ 963.60
Ending Inventory	50	301.00	50	300.90	50	301.04	50	300.10
	210	$1,263.70	210	$1,263.70	210	$1,263.70	210	$1,263.70

5.7 to illustrate the LIFO pricing procedure. The ending balance is made up of 45 units at $6.00 (the oldest or first price) and 5 units at $6.05 (the newest price) for a total of $300.10.

The Effect on Cost under These Pricing Systems

Now that the mechanics of the various pricing systems have been discussed, the effect of these systems on costs can be explored. Table 5.8 presents the preceding data in abbreviated form. It can be seen that in all systems there are 210 units available at a cost of $1,263.70.

Table 5.9

		Units	Dollars per Unit	Goods Available Units	Goods Available Dollars	Sales Units	Sales Dollars
Jan. 1	Beginning Balance	1,000	20	1,000	20,000		
Jan. 30	Sold	700	30			700	21,000
Feb. 12	Purchased	1,200	22	1,200	26,400		
Feb. 28	Sold	900	33			900	29,700
Mar. 9	Purchased	800	24	800	19,200		
March. 31	Sold	700	36			700	25,200
				3,000	65,600	2,300	75,900

Table 5.10(a) FIFO pricing.

Jan.	700 u. @ $20		$14,000
Feb.	300 u. @ $20	$ 6,000	
	600 u. @ $22	13,200	19,200
Mar.	600 u. @ $22	13,200	
	100 u. @ $24	2,400	15,600
Cost of goods sold			$48,800

Table 5.10(b) Average pricing.

Average cost:
$$\frac{\$65,600}{3,000 \text{ u.}} = \$21.87/\text{u.}$$
Cost of goods sold (2,300 u. @ $21.87)　　　　$50,301

Table 5.10(c) Moving-average pricing.

	Purchases		Usage		Balance		
	Units	Amount	Units	Amount	Units	Cost/unit	Amount
Jan.1 Opening balance					1,000	$20.00	$20,000
Jan. 31 Usage			700	$14,000	300		6,000
Feb. 12 Purchase	1,200	$26,400			1,500	$21.60	32,400
Feb. 28 Usage			900	19,440	600		12,960
Mar. 9 Purchase	800	19,200			1,400	$22.97	32,160
Mar. 29 Usage			700	16,079	700		16,081
Cost of goods sold			2,300	$49,519			

However, the amount charged to production varies from a low for FIFO of $962.70 to a high for LIFO of $963.60, with the average and moving average in between. This will always be so in periods of rising prices. Since over the past century there has been a general tendency to rising price levels, LIFO will produce the lowest profit and the lowest ending inventory.

The Income Tax Effect of the Various Pricing Systems

There is a significant tax effect due to pricing under the various pricing systems. This is illustrated by the data in Tables 5.9, 5.10, and 5.11, based on purchases and sales of a finished product, although the same effect filters through a manufacturing process.

Note in Table 5.9 that in all cases the total goods available are always 3,000 units, costing $65,600, and the total sales are always $75,900. The method of determining the cost of goods sold, however, depends on the pricing system used, as Tables 5.10(a) through 5.10(d) show.

A comparison of data in Tables 5.10(a) through 5.10(d) provides a basis for the Income Statement. A summary of these comparative data is given in Table 5.11.

Assuming this is a corporation that has income in excess of $25,000,

Table 5.10(d) LIFO pricing.

Jan. 700 u. @ $20	$14,000
Feb. 900 u. @ $22	19,800
Mar. 700 u. @ $24	16,800
Cost of goods sold	$50,600

Table 5.11

	FIFO	Average	Moving Average	LIFO
Sales	$75,900	$75,900	$75,900	$75,900
Cost of goods sold	48,800	50,301	49,519	50,600
Gross profit	$27,100	$25,599	$26,381	$25,300
Profit as compared to FIFO:		$ 1,501 less	$ 719 less	$ 1,800 less

therefore being taxed 48 percent (normal tax of 22 percent and surtax of 26 percent on income over $25,000), the federal income tax savings over the income tax figured using FIFO are:

Average	$720
Moving average	$345
LIFO	$864

Add to these figures any savings in state taxes based on income, and it can be readily seen that the tax savings will be substantial and may be used by the company as a source of present financing at no cost. Remember, however, since profits in the same company are ultimately equal, regardless of the inventory method used, in the long run this nonpayment of income taxes will result in greater income tax payments at some time in the future (assuming constant tax rates).

QUESTIONS

1. A company has a beginning raw materials inventory of $27,000, purchases (net) of $290,000, and an ending inventory of $32,000. What is the cost of materials used in production?

2. The following data relate to Item 602 B in the inventory of Oxypal Co.

Jan. 1	Opening inventory	600 u @ $10
Jan. 31	Usage	500 u.
Feb. 6	Purchase	700 u. @ $11
Feb. 28	Usage	400 u.
Mar. 15	Purchase	500 u. @ $12
Mar. 15	Usage	700 u.

(a) What is the cost of the materials used in the first quarter—using the FIFO, average, moving-average, and LIFO pricing systems? (b) What is the ending inventory under each of these pricing systems?

Factory Overhead

As previously stated, factory overhead consists of all factory costs other than direct labor and direct materials. There are some problems that might arise with labor when production personnel cannot, for whatever reasons, work at their production station and are either idle or are temporarily transferred to nonproduction work. The cost of this nonproductive time must be separated from production costs and properly charged to factory overhead. Other problems arise with direct materials. One such problem is created by the insignificant amounts of direct materials used in production (thread used in sewing a book, etc.), which for accounting simplicity are charged to factory overhead. Another problem arises when production material is used for maintenance and repairs (nuts, bolts, and other small common parts). Where the factory site houses administrative and/or sales functions, allocation of costs must be made, and this also presents a problem.

THE FACTORY OVERHEAD ACCOUNT

Factory overhead is one of the accounts in the General Ledger, which collects all factory overhead costs. For purposes of control these costs should be collected by responsibility centers (superintendent's office, cost accounting department, repair and maintenance department, power department, etc.), and should be segregated according to functional category (light and power, heat, telephone, water, taxes, etc.). The first classification permits pinpointing the spending responsibility and allows the report data given to department heads to be broken down into controllable and uncontrollable costs. For example, the cost of salaries is controllable by the department head, whereas the prorated cost of the power plant charged to the department is not controllable if the total power-plant costs are allocated to the department on a predetermined (not currently measured) basis. Any savings in the power-plant department are, in effect, distributed to all departments just as excess costs would be.

When costs are collected by function, the total of the functional cost from one period to another can be analyzed to ascertain trends in costs. This helps to pinpoint inefficient use of the function measured, or assists in developing projections and budget data for future periods.

Indirect Labor

All factory labor not used in actually producing the product is indirect labor. This includes all gross wages of personnel from the superintendent to the sweepers and warehouse laborers. These persons are, in the main, assigned to a factory department and make the charging of costs fairly simple.

The wages of a working foreman who supervises and also produces the product require allocation of cost, as do those of the production worker who is temporarily transferred to a nonproduction assignment.

All fringe benefits of both direct and indirect factory labor are a factory overhead cost. These include the employer's portion of Social Security and Medicare taxes, unemployment insurance (both federal and state), and Workmen's Compensation insurance. They also include vacation pay and paid time-off. Also included are the other fringe benefits described in Chapter 3. For purposes of control these fringe benefits should be collected by category so that the trend of the specific items may be analyzed and some evaluation made of their effectiveness.

Indirect Materials

All material not used directly in producing the product is indirect material. This includes all costs for materials used by janitorial personnel, and the repair and maintenance personnel, among others.

These materials might be stored in general storerooms or in departmental storerooms. The latter may be advantageous because the department head takes responsibility for having the proper materials needed on hand and for maintaining the inventory at the proper levels. He is familiar with the items and their rate of usage, knows the supply sources and the delivery times, etc., and can assist the purchasing agent in the procurement of these materials.

When a department draws materials from regular stores, the proper charge should be made to the department by the issuing storeroom. This will insure the control necessary to prevent misuse and theft of commonly used items.

Purchases of Other Goods or Services

Most of the factory overhead costs (other than indirect labor and indirect materials) are recognized in the records of the company when an invoice is received. The company has some way of checking the validity of the invoice before paying it. A common method used is the voucher system. When the invoice is received, a clerk prepares a voucher showing the vendor and the accounting distribution of the charge. This is approved before it is entered in the accounting records. The person approving the charge will initial or sign the voucher, making him responsible for the validity of the charge.

Many of the invoices are for continuing services like utilities and telephone. Here the approver checks to see if the charge is reasonably related to past experience and his knowledge of activity changes within the factory.

Some charges are fixed or under outside control, such as rent or taxes. Here the approver verifies amounts and investigates any changes. The approver also checks the distribution of the charge to the factory, administration, and sales. He may also review allocation formulas and adjust them when the premises upon which they were developed change. This review is most important in making sure that the allocation of charges reflects the current percentage of benefits.

The approval of the voucher and its distribution is a responsibility function and should be assigned to someone with authority in the accounting department. This person should have knowledge of the company and its activities, and should be continually updating that knowledge by receiving essential plant documents, by having a good rapport with production and nonproduction department heads, and by touring the premises to see what the activities are and how they are changing.

Allocation of Prepaid Items

Most companies have prepaid expense items on the books. These include premiums for insurance of various kinds on the plant and equipment, damage of material or machinery, fire, theft, etc. At some time in the period the accounting department allocates these items to production by internal transfer from prepaid assets to cost (called an "adjusting journal entry"). Other such items may be allocation of patent and franchise costs, and the expensing and allocation of research and development costs. Prepaid interest costs may be also included.

For insurance purposes the amount of the charge may be a time analysis based on the term of the policy; for patents, a time analysis based on the legal or economic life of the patent; for franchises, a time or production unit analysis; for interest, an analysis of interest cost based on loan balances and the length of the loan.

Allocation of Plant Assets

One of the large investments of a manufacturing company is that made in buildings, equipment, fixtures, and other assets of long duration. Although these assets must be purchased at a specific time, their economic utility extends over many future periods, and their usage must be computed by rational, mathematical allocation formulas and individually charged and spread over expected economic or physical life, whichever is shorter. This allocation process is called "depreciation."

Since an asset is acquired at a specific time, its entire cost is set up as an asset when purchased. Whether it is paid for at the time of purchase, at a later date, or in a series of installments over a relatively short period of time does not affect the fact that it is an asset.

Accountants recognize that all plant assets (except land) lose their economic effectiveness over time. It is the periodic depreciation of its economic effectiveness that is charged as an expense during a stated period. The accountant must make some judgments before he can determine how much to charge each period. The judgments include:

1. *The cost of the asset.* This includes the invoice price plus costs of freight, carrier insurance, and transport to the plant, and the cost

of setting up the asset ready to operate. In the case of a building purchased with the site, a breakdown is made between land and building purchase prices. The land is set up as a nondepreciable asset and the building is set up as a depreciable asset. The total cost is derived from the escrow document developed for the purchaser; those costs that are building-related are charged to building, and the remainder of the costs are prorated between land and building on an equitable basis. The proration may be based on an appraisal of the property by an appraiser, or the tax-bill assessment values for land and improvements may be used.

2. *The economic life of the asset.* This is an estimate of how long the asset is expected to be used in production. In the case of a jig or fixture used to make a part and which is redesigned on some regular basis, the economic life is the length of time between redesigns, and may well be related to the number of units expected to be produced.

3. *The physical life of the asset.* This estimate is related to durability; that is, how long the asset will last before it wears out and can no longer serve the purposes for which it was built. An adjustment factor may be allowed if repair and maintenance procedures during this period will keep it in good working order and thereby extend its useful life.

4. *Selection of the shorter of the economic or physical life for depreciation purposes.* To assist in this selection of plant asset lives, the Internal Revenue Service has established (for assets purchased after 1970) the Class Life Asset Depreciation Range (ADR), showing asset by class with an ADR (in years) of a lower limit and upper limit (among other data). As long as the life selected falls within this range, there should be no question of its acceptability. If a shorter life than the lower limit is used, there must be sufficient reason to justify this shorter life.

5. *Determination of the salvage value at the end of asset life.* This requires a projection of what may be salvageable at the end of the life selected.

The cost to be charged to operations over the life selected is

$$\text{Cost at site ready to use} - \text{salvage value}$$

In more sophisticated analyses, the salvage value used in this formula is the present value of the salvage value at the end of the economic life. There are several ways to arrive at this value. For example: An asset costs $21,000 + $1,500 to install ready for use. It is estimated that its economic life (which is shorter than its physical life) is ten years. At the end of the economic life, it is *estimated* that the asset can be sold for $2,500.

The accountant might want to set up a cost of $20,000 ($22,500 − $2,500) to depreciate. (The amount of yearly depreciation will be discussed below.) However, another analysis, for other purposes, might show that today the asset would cost $21,695.

Cash outlay now	$22,500
Present value of salvage, assuming a 12% interest rate ($2,500 × 0.322)	805
	$21,695

Note: 0.322 is the present value factor for 12 percent for ten years.

The analysis is saying that the present outlay is $21,695, since to receive $2,500 ten years from now, an amount of $805 must be invested at 12 percent.

Both the accountant and the analyst are correct in their own way. However, the accountant stays with his figure because the $2,500 salvage value is an estimate, the ten-year economic life is an estimate, and the 12 percent interest rate for the ten years is an estimate. And the difference between $20,000 and $21,695 is only 8 percent, which will not materially affect the profits of any year when spread over ten years. The accountant likes to have as few assumptions or estimates as possible in his calculations, and the profession has traditionally not used discounted values. Therefore the prevalent statement presentation would be $20,000 spread over the ten years.

Depreciation Methods for Fixed Assets

In developing a formula for charging the $20,000 to current and future operations, the accountant has four methods from which to choose:

1. *Straight line (SL).* This method is based on the premise that time is the major factor in loss of asset usefulness, and that each time period should be charged the same amount of cost as any other period.

2. *Per unit.* This method is based on the premise that each unit produced uses up an equal amount of the asset's economic life, and that the charge to current and future operations will vary as production varies.

3. *Declining balance (DB).* This method is based on the premise

that the real cost of using an asset is the economic loss in life plus maintenance costs. In the early years the maintenance costs are low, but they increase over time. Therefore, to equalize the continued charge to current and future operations over the economic life, the depreciation is "speeded up" in the earlier years. This method of graduating depreciation is popular because of its effect on income taxes.

4. *Sum-of-the-years' digits (SYD)*. This has the same premise as declining balance, but uses a different formula. It is also popular because of its effect on income taxes.

The formulas used in these various methods are as follows:

1. *Straight line*

$$\frac{\text{Asset cost} - \text{salvage value}}{\text{Periods of economic or physical life}} = \text{depreciation expense/period}$$

2. *Per unit*

$$\frac{\text{Asset cost} - \text{salvage value}}{\text{Estimated units of production}}$$

$$= \text{depreciation expense/unit of production}$$

and then

(Depreciation expense/unit of production) × (number of units produced in period) = depreciation expense for period

3. *Declining balance*

$$\frac{100\%}{\text{Number of periods of life}} = \text{depreciation rate/period}$$

Then this rate is multiplied by the allowable factor (200, 150, or 125 percent, depending on asset type, etc., as allowed under the Internal Revenue Code) to get the rate used for computation, which is applied to the book value of the asset to determine the depreciation expense for the period.

4. *Sum-of-the-years' digits*. The sums of all years in the asset's life are added. This figure becomes the denominator of a fraction. The numerator is the year of life of the asset (in descending order). This fraction is multiplied by the (cost – salvage value) to get the depreciation expense for the period.

Examples: Assume an asset costing $32,000 has a salvage value of $2,000 and an asset life of ten years (for purposes of unit depreciation, 100,000 units).

Straight line

$$\frac{\text{Cost} - \text{salvage value}}{\text{Number of periods}} = \frac{\$32,000 - \$2,000}{10 \text{ years}} = \$3,000 \text{ per year}$$

Per unit

$$\frac{\text{Cost} - \text{salvage value}}{\text{Number of units}} = \frac{\$32,000 - \$2,000}{100,000 \text{ units}} = \$0.30 \text{ per unit}$$

See Table 6.1.

Table 6.1

Year	Units Produced	Depreciation Expense	Accumulated Depreciation
19A	5,000	$1,500	$ 1,500
B	7,000	2,100	3,600
C	12,000	3,600	7,200
D	14,000	4,200	11,400
E	19,000	5,700	17,100
F	15,000	4,500	21,600
G	10,000	3,000	24,600
H	9,000	2,700	27,300
I	5,000	1,500	28,800
J	4,000+	1,200	30,000

Note: Only the total of $30,000 can be depreciated, although over 100,000 units are produced.

Table 6.2

	Book Value (1)	Accumulated Depreciation (2)	Depreciation Expense (3) = 15% × (1)
Cost	$32,000		
19A	27,200	$ 4,800	$4,800
B	23,120	8,880	4,080
C	19,652	12,348	3,468
D	16,704	15,296	2,948
E	14,198	17,802	2,506
F	12,068	19,932	2,130
G	10,258	21,742	1,810
H	8,719	23,281	1,539
I	7,411	24,589	1,308
J	6,299	25,701	1,112

Declining balance (150%)

$$\frac{100\%}{10 \text{ years}} = 10\% \text{ per year}$$

$$10\% \times 150\% = 15\%$$

See Table 6.2.

To bring the book value to salvage value by the end of the tenth year, the schedule is sometimes modified to take an equal charge in the later years. The modified schedule might be as shown in Table 6.3.

Sum-of-the-Years' Digits

$$10 + 9 + 8 + 7 + 6 + 5 + 4 + 3 + 2 + 1 = 55 \text{ (denominator)}$$

$$\text{Cost} - \text{salvage value} = \$30,000$$

See Table 6.4.

Table 6.3

Year	Book Value	Accumulated Depreciation	Depreciation Expense
19E	$14,198	$17,802	$2,506
F	11,758	20,242	2,440
G	9,318	22,682	2,440
H	6,878	25,122	2,440
I	4,438	25,562	2,440
J	2,000	30,000	2,438

Table 6.4

Year	Fraction	Depreciation Expense	Accumulated Depreciation
19A	10/55	$5,454	$ 5,454
B	9/55	4,909	10,363
C	8/55	4,364	14,727
D	7/55	3,818	18,545
E	6/55	3,273	21,818
F	5/55	2,727	24,545
G	4/55	2,182	26,727
H	3/55	1,636	28,363
I	2/55	1,091	29,454
J	1/55	546	30,000

Figure 6.1 is a graph of the preceding data. It can be seen that the depreciation expense pattern is significantly different, year by year, under each method. If these data were to be plotted on a cumulative basis, the resulting graph would be like Figure 6.2.

The effects of these different methods under the premise and conditions described can be summarized as follows: Straight-line

Figure 6.1   Depreciation expense per year.

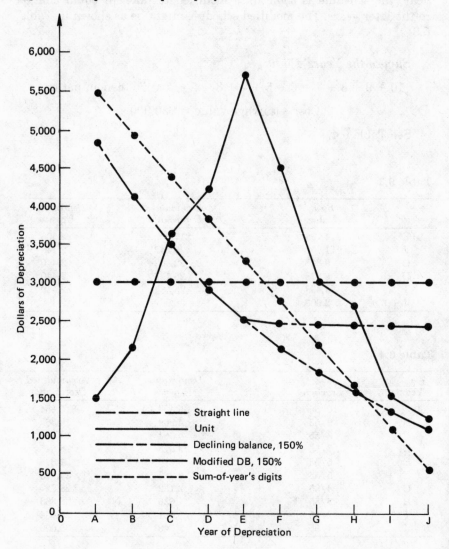

Figure 6.2 Cumulative depreciation expense.

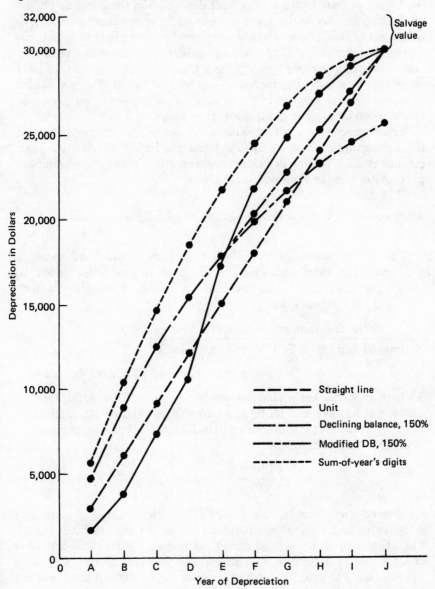

depreciation is simple and is easiest to use, but it does not vary with production output. Therefore, as production varies and the depreciation expense remains constant, the gross profit percentage from year to year changes. Per-unit depreciation tends to match the production and keeps the gross margin-profit percentage more in line with cost of sales. The accelerated methods (modified declining balance and sum-of-the-years' digits) charge greater expenses in the earlier years, reducing income (and income taxes) in those years; in later years they create higher incomes (and income taxes). This tends also to lessen the risk involved in new plant, new processes, etc., because of the income tax savings in the earlier years.

The depreciation method selected by management (perhaps with the accountant's advice) can affect the profitabilities year by year, can affect sales pricing decisions, and can affect plant and equipment purchasing and/or replacement decisions.

Allocation of Factory Overhead to Production

The actual overhead is collected in factory overhead expense accounts. Then these expenses are allocated to production (work in process) on a formula basis. The formula used to develop the factory overhead rate (burden rate) is

$$\frac{\text{Estimated factory overhead (\$)}}{\text{Estimated number of FOH distribution units}}$$

$$= \text{burden rate expressed as \$/distribution unit}$$

Assume that the estimated factory overhead will be $150,000 and that direct labor hours (DLH) input correlates highly with productive output. It is estimated that there will be 50,000 DLH used in production. The burden rate then is

$$\frac{\$150,000}{50,000 \text{ DLH}} = \$3/\text{DLH}$$

As production proceeds, the direct labor hours actually used are collected (along with direct materials costs and direct labor costs). Then the total of the actual direct labor hours is multiplied by the burden rate to determine the amount of overhead to be charged to the product. For example, in the current month 700 units of product X were started and completed, consuming 500 direct labor hours. The data collected are listed in Table 6.5.

Table 6.5

	Total	Per Unit
Direct labor	$2,100	$ 3.000
Direct materials	4,900	7.000
Burden:		
500 DLH × ($3/DLH)	1,500	2.143
Total cost	$8,500	$12.143

Over- and Under-Applied Overhead and Its Disposition

As can be seen from the overhead distribution formula, the rate is based on estimates of costs and estimates of distribution units, and then the rate is applied to actual distribution units to get the charge to be made to production. It is apparent that the actual factory overhead and the applied factory overhead cannot be the same, but the difference (when measured as a percentage of total product cost) should be small. This small difference is closed out to the Cost of Goods Sold account for the period.

ANALYSIS OF FACTORY OVERHEAD

The accountant generally analyzes the factory overhead charges by type of charge; for example, superintendent's office salaries, utilities, telephone, and insurance. This is sometimes described as "analysis by line item." The purpose of this is to allow for comparison of the actual costs with the estimated cost used to develop the factory overhead rate. The analysis of factory overhead variance will be discussed in Chapter 10.

Departmental Factory Overhead Rates

In some plants there may not be a common basis that has a high correlation with production in all productive departments of the plant. Assume a plant prepares parts by machine, paints them in a department operated by a few persons who spray-paint the parts, and assembles the parts by hand in the last department. In this example the bases for distribution of factory overhead might be machine hours, gallons of paint, and direct labor hours.

To develop the overhead rates, the overhead may be analyzed by

Table 6.6

	Estimated Factory Overhead	Estimated Number of Distribution Units
Machine Department	$100,000	20,000 machine hours
Paint Department	75,000	12,000 gallons of paint
Assembly Department	55,000	10,000 direct labor hours

department. The factory overhead by department and the distribution units in each department are used to calculate departmental overhead rates, which are then multiplied by the actual distribution units to get the charge applicable to each department. To develop this example, we use the data in Table 6.6. Then the developed factory overhead rates are:

Machine department	$5.00/machine hour
Paint department	$6.25/gallon of paint
Assembly department	$5.50/direct labor hour

Service Department Costs and Dispositions

Those departments in the factory that are not product-producing are called "service" departments. They include the plant manager's office, plant accounting office, quality control department, plant maintenance department, power department, etc. All service groups accumulate costs, and sometimes these costs are allocated directly to production when the work they perform is essentially a collateral production function. Examples of concomitant services would be the percentage of inspector's time spent in inspecting the output of the production department or the power department output used by the production department.

Assume a plant with three producing departments (A, B, and C) and three service departments (general factory, storeroom, and maintenance). The direct overhead costs prior to allocation of service department costs are: Dept. A, $40,000; Dept. B, $50,000; Dept. C, $55,000; general factory, $70,000; storeroom, $15,000; maintenance department, $25,000. It has been decided to distribute these costs as follows:

1. General factory costs to the production department on the basis of direct labor dollars: Dept. A, $15,000; Dept. B, $10,000; Dept. C, $10,000.

Table 6.7 Factory overhead distribution.

	Dept. A	Dept. B	Dept. C	General Factory	Storeroom	Maintenance	Total
Costs before allocation	$40,000	$50,000	$55,000	$70,000	$15,000	$25,000	$255,000
Allocate general factory (15/35; 10/35; 10/35)	30,000	20,000	20,000	($70,000)			
Allocate storeroom (175/300; 75/300; 50/300)	8,750	3,750	2,500		($15,000)		
Allocate maintenance (3/10; 2/10; 5/10)	7,500	5,000	12,500			($25,000)	
Costs after allocation	$86,250	$78,750	$90,000				$255,000

Table 6.8 Departmental cost allocations.

	Dept. A	Dept. B	Dept. C	Service Dept. 1	Service Dept. 2	Service Dept. 3	Total
Costs before allocation	$ 60,000	$ 75,000	$ 80,000	$ 97,000	$77,500	$50,000	$439,500
Close out Service Dept. 3 (40%; 30%; 15%; 10%; 5%)	20,000	15,000	7,500	5,000	2,500	(50,000)	
					80,000		
Close out Service Dept. 2 (35%; 40%; 15%; 10%)	28,000	32,000	12,000	8,000	(80,000)		
				110,000			
Close out Service Dept. 1 (35%; 35%; 30%)	38,500	38,500	33,000	(110,000)			
Costs after allocation	$146,500	$160,500	$132,500				$439,500

2. Storeroom costs on the basis of dollars of inventory requisitioned from the storeroom: Dept. A, $175,000; Dept. B, $75,000; Dept. C, $50,000.
3. Maintenance costs on the basis of hours spent in each production department: Dept. A, 3,000 hours; Dept. B, 2,000 hours; Dept. C, 5,000 hours.

The schedule used to record the total factory overhead for the production departments is given in Table 6.7.

During the year overhead would have been applied by department, based on accumulation of actual distribution units. The difference between actual and applied departmental overhead would be closed out to the Cost of Goods Sold account, as previously noted.

Another way to close out costs of service departments to production departments is to rank the service departments. Then all costs of the first-ranking service department are closed to all other service departments and the production departments. The costs of the second-ranking service department are closed to all remaining service departments and the production departments; and so forth until all service departments are closed out.

The listing of allocations might look like Table 6.8.

QUESTIONS

1. A company has direct materials costs of $500,000 and direct labor costs of $600,000 to produce 100,000 units per year. The overhead is $1,400,000. It is estimated that the net cost of a leased computer to be used in the plant for scheduling, inventory control, etc., would be $50,000 per year. (a) What is the effect on profits for the year; (b) on burden rate based on direct labor dollars for the year; and (c) on per-unit cost?

2. At a meeting with top production management personnel the controller said, "We should review the position descriptions of all indirect personnel and do a management audit of their effectiveness." What effect could such a program have on firm profitability?

3. In looking at a manufactured article selling for $25, it can be readily ascertained by the purchaser that the direct materials costs are in the range of $2 to $3 and that the direct labor costs are in the range of $4 to $7. Yet he cannot estimate the factory overhead cost per unit as readily. Why is that?

4. Given an asset cost of $43,000, a salvage value of $3,000, and an asset

life of 10 years, compute the depreciation expense for the first three years under: (a) straight line, (b) declining balance (assume 150 percent), and (c) sum-of-the-years' digits.

5. It is estimated that total factory overhead will be $190,000 for next year and the total direct labor will be 50,000 hours. What is the factory overhead rate?

6. The factory overhead rate is 150 percent of direct labor dollars. In Dept. 3, the total amount of direct labor dollars is $120,000. How much factory overhead should be charged to Dept. 3?

7. A schedule of depreciation charges for the first two years of a fixed asset is given below. (a) Which method gives the lowest profit? (b) How would you do this? (c) Assuming a 47 percent income tax rate, how much taxes are saved the first two years?

	Year 1	Year 2
Straight line	$45,000	$45,000
Declining balance (150%)	72,000	61,200
Sum-of-the-years' digits	81,810	73,635

Cost-Volume—
Profit Relationship

A good way to understand firm profitability is to look at the relationship between cost and volume. Common sense tells us that as the volume of sales increases, income increases; as the volume of production increases, cost increases. From an analytical standpoint, however, this is too simplistic and totally inadequate. Our concern is with the rates of increase over volume.

The basic model for cost-volume-profit analysis consists of one product and assumes that all that is produced is sold. It also assumes that certain costs are the same over the whole range of production (*fixed costs*) and that another set of costs varies directly with production (*variable costs*), and further that sales income varies directly with units sold. These relationships are graphically represented by Figure 7.1.

The total sales income is expressed as

$$(\text{Sales price/unit}) \times \text{number of units sold}$$

or

$$(S/u) \times Q$$

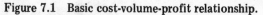

Figure 7.1 Basic cost-volume-profit relationship.

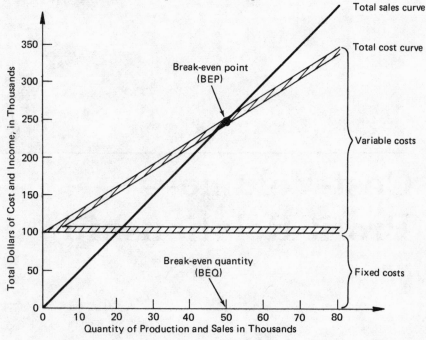

Figure 7.2 Contribution margin cost-volume-profit relationship.

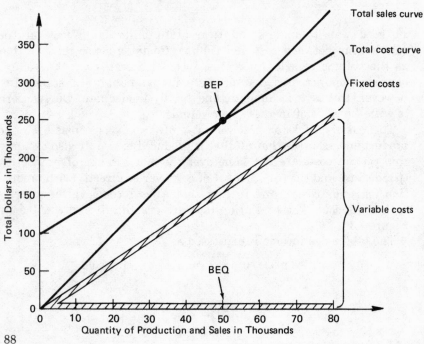

The total cost is expressed as

Fixed cost + (variable cost/unit) × number of units produced

or

$$FC + (VC/u) \times Q$$

Where the total cost and the total sales curves cross is the *break-even point* (BEP), and the quantity at that point is called the *break-even quantity* (BEQ). From zero quantity to BEQ, the firm loses money; from BEQ and beyond, the firm makes money. To solve for the break-even quantity, one has only to set the income formula equal to the total cost formula and solve for Q.

Some of those accountants studying these relationships devised another way of looking at cost behavior. By reversing the order of the fixed and the variable cost and by looking at unit 1, they developed the *contribution margin* analysis. Using the same data given for Figure 7.1, the graph of Figure 7.2 assists in this analysis.

If we graph the cost and sales data for the first unit produced and sold (Figure 7.3), we shall get a clearer picture of what is happening to costs and income. From Figure 7.2 it can be seen that at 50,000 units, sales are $250,000 (or $5.00 per unit); fixed costs are $100,000; and variable costs at 50,000 units are $150,000 (or $3.00 per unit). Using the same trend curves as those for unit 1, it can be readily seen that the first unit (and all other units) "contribute" $2.00 ($5.00 − $3.00) to the firm. This $2.00 contribution is first used to offset fixed costs (up to the breakdown point) and is then added to the profitability beyond that point.

As a result of this analysis, the computation is simplified:

$$\text{BEQ} = \frac{\text{fixed costs}}{\text{contribution margin}}$$

In the author's opinion this still did not clarify the relationship because per-unit cost behavior should be analyzed.

By using the data of Figure 7.1, but plotting them on a *per-unit* basis, the graph in Figure 7.4 is developed.

An examination of Figure 7.4 shows that in the lower volumes, per-unit costs drop rapidly, but in the higher volumes, per-unit costs tend to flatten out or not change so much. This tells a lot to the manager.

1. The smaller the fixed costs, the less the BEP will be (cutting fixed costs from $100,000 to $80,000 will reduce the BEP from 50,000 to 40,000 units).

Figure 7.3 Contribution analysis of unit 1.

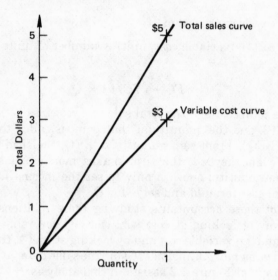

Figure 7.4 Per-unit cost-volume-profit relationship.

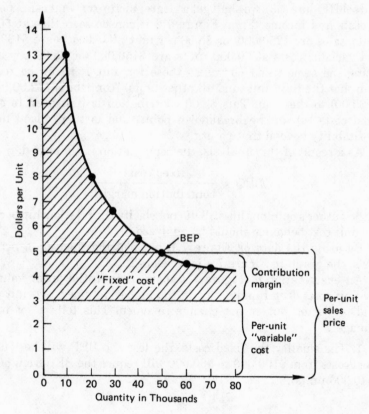

2. Each unit beyond the BEP contributes a little more to profit, not only for itself, but also for all units before it. Let us look at the profit for 60,000 units in total:

Sales, 60,000 × $5.00		$300,000
Fixed costs	$100,000	
Variable costs, 60,000 × $3.00	180,000	280,000
Total profit		20,000

On a per-unit basis (60,000 units):

Sales		$5.0000000
Fixed costs, ($100,000)/60,000	$1.6666667	
Variable costs	3.0000000	4.6666667
Unit profit at 60,000		$0.3333333
Total profit (60,000 × 0.3333333)		$20,000

On a per-unit basis (60,001 units):

Sales		$5.0000000
Fixed costs, ($100,000)/60,001	$1.6666388	
Variable costs	3.0000000	4.6666388
Unit profit at 60,001		$0.3333612
Total profit (60,001 × 0.3333612)		$20,002

The $2.00 in extra profit is made up of the drop in per-unit cost of $0.0000279 ($4.6666667 − $4.6666388) times 60,001 units. All prior units benefit from the production and sale of the extra unit.

RELEVANT RANGE

At this point it might be profitable to examine one of the assumptions made at the beginning of this chapter, namely, that fixed costs are the same over the whole range of production. What any good manager knows is that the plant will not be operated below some level because of fixed costs, and cannot be operated above some other level because of physical and policy constraints. In our preceding example the lower limit might be set at 40,000 units and the upper limit at 70,000 units (although it might be theoretically possible to produce 80,000 units, if there were no inefficiencies). The relevant

Figure 7.5 Examples of nonproduction total cost behavior.

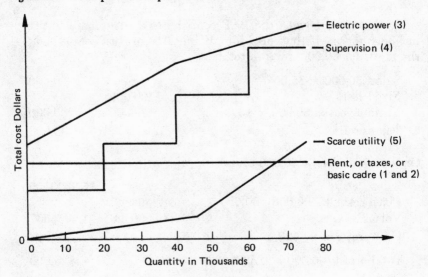

Figure 7.6 Multiple product cost-volume-profit relationship.

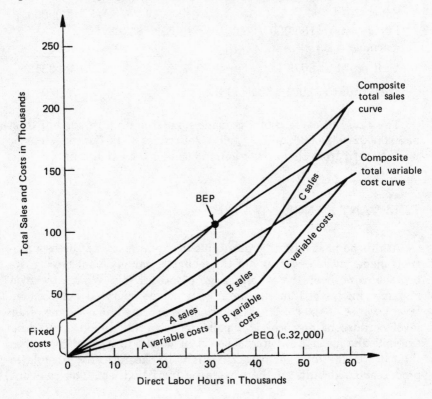

range then is 40,000 to 70,000 units. The fixed costs are then established at $100,000 over this range and the subsequent analyses demonstrated above will be made.

Fixed Cost Behavior

In the real world the "fixed" costs may well increase with increased volume. Examination of some of these costs might show the following results (see Figure 7.5):

1. Rent or property taxes are truly fixed; they do not vary with production.
2. A cadre of people in the plant will be fixed in number and in salary.
3. Some indirect costs increase slower than production increases. An example might be electric power, for which the rate per kilowatt-hour reduces as more is used.
4. Some indirect costs increase in step fashion. An example would be the addition of an additional supervisor on the production floor where a certain level of production employees had been reached.
5. Some indirect costs increase more rapidly than production increases. An example would be increased per-unit cost of a scarce utility as more units are purchased.

It can be seen in Figure 7.5 that, even in the relevant range, the costs are not constant, but are fluctuating at varying rates relative to production increase. An analysis of the elements of costs, which were described originally in the analysis as "fixed" costs, will give the manager a better set of data upon which to base his decisions.

Table 7.1

Product	Sales in Units	Sales Price/ Unit	Total Sales	Variable Cost/ Unit	Total Variable Cost	Direct Labor Hours to Produce One Unit	Total Direct Labor Hours
A	10,000	$ 5	$ 50,000	$ 3	$ 30,000	3.0	30,000
B	5,000	6	30,000	5	25,000	2.0	10,000
C	8,000	15	120,000	11	88,000	2.5	20,000
Total			$200,000		$143,000		60,000

In far too many cases in talking to managers at all levels of production, the author has found a hazy knowledge of cost behavior. Perhaps some have a good knowledge of total cost and profitability for a given level of production and sales, based on past performance, but have a poor knowledge of current per-unit cost behaviors and their effects on profitability.

One other assumption was made at the beginning of this chapter: there was *one* product. In reality there may be more than one product. However, the basic analysis still holds true, but we must revise the graph to account for two or more products. First, the quantity dimension must be put in another form; direct labor hours might be a good measure. Second, the mix of sales must be known and a composite "product" must be devised. The variable cost of the composite product is developed. For this analysis, use the data in Table 7.1 as the bases for the graph in Figure 7.6 (fixed costs are $30,000).

It can be seen from Figure 7.6 that the break-even quantity is reached at about 32,000 direct labor hours. Solving this mathematically (assuming the mix of sales and production holds constant throughout the period), we compute

$$\text{Total sales price}/\text{DLH} = \frac{\$200,000}{60,000 \text{ DLH}} = \$3.333$$

$$\text{Total variable cost}/\text{DLH} = \frac{\$143,000}{60,000 \text{ DLH}} = \underline{\$2.383}$$

$$\text{Contribution margin} \qquad\qquad\qquad \underline{\underline{\$0.95/\text{DLH}}}$$

$$\text{Break-even quantity} = \frac{\$30,000}{\$0.95/\text{DLH}} = 31,579 \text{ units}$$

QUESTIONS

1. Are fixed costs always the same over the total range of production? If not, why are they called "fixed"?

2. What is contribution margin analysis?

3. What is the break-even point?

4. Given the following facts, determine the break-even quantity:
   Sales at 40,000 units are $240,000
   Variable costs at 40,000 units are $160,000
   Fixed costs are $40,000

5. Given the following facts, determine the break-even quantity:

     Sales, $7/unit; variable costs, $4/unit; fixed costs, $15,000

6. Using examples other than those discussed in this chapter, draw graphs for fixed costs that change in total dollars over the production range.

7. Determine mathematically the break-even quantity from the following data (fixed costs are $125,000):

Product	Sales in Units	Sales Price/Unit	Variable Cost/Unit	Direct Labor Hours/Unit
A	20,000	$15,00	$ 7.50	4
B	15,000	10.00	7.00	2
C	10,000	20.00	16.00	3

8

Standard Costs

SINCE prices of materials put into production may vary in price per unit from purchase to purchase, and the cost of labor per hour may vary because of the different wage rates of the persons who might be assigned to a task, the historical method of costing will arrive at differing prices for the manufactured product.

RATIONALE FOR STANDARD COST

Standard cost accounting is based on the proposition that there is a given amount of material in a product and a given amount of labor in a product, and that in a given period of time, prices tend to vary around some "average" price per unit or per hour. It is fairly easy to see that in bidding for a job, such an analysis must be made to arrive at the price to a customer before production starts—in fact, before the order is secured. Production is charged with the standard cost of making the unit while (for materials) the Raw Materials Inventory account is relieved of the actual cost. The difference goes to the Materials Quantity Variance account and the Materials Price Variance account.

For direct labor, production is charged with standard cost while the Labor Summary account is relieved of the actual cost. The difference goes to the Labor Hours Variance account and the Labor Rate Variance account.

Standard Cost Illustration: Material

In a study of how many units of A are required to produce a lot of 500 units of part 202, experience shows that 510 units of A have been used (one of A for each item in the lot plus a 2 percent spoilage of A). It is also found that the price of item A varies from $1.75 to $1.82 each, and that a weighted average of the prices over the past year is $1.80 per item A. The standards to produce a lot of 500 units of Part 202 might then be set at 510 units of item A at $1.80 per unit, or $918.00. This is diagrammed in Figure 8.1.

However, to produce 500 units of part A in a production run, 507 units of item A are used at a cost of $1.81 per unit, or $917.67. The total difference between standard ($918.00) and actual ($917.67) is very small, producing a savings of 0.04 percent. Yet management wants to know about the variance, as small as it is, so that it can take remedial action in areas where there is a tendency to increase cost and institute procedural changes where there is a tendency to decrease cost.

VARIANCE ANALYSIS

To subtract actual cost from standard cost gives a figure that includes both quantity and price variance. This figure is made up of a favorable or unfavorable quantity variance and of a favorable or unfavorable price variance. What are the variances?

Using the format of Figure 8.1 and entering the actual data, we obtain Figure 8.2. From Figure 8.2 it can be seen that the standard cost of $918.00 has been modified by an increase of $5.07 (due to a one-cent price increase for 507 units) and by a decrease of $5.40 (due to a usage reduction of three units at $1.80 each), for a total actual cost of $917.67.

Accountants have developed a simple way to analyze the difference. They start out with actual units used, times actual cost per unit. Then they change one of the factors (price or quantity) to standard. The difference gives the variance due to the factor that was changed. The remaining difference is the variance due to the other factor.

Figure 8.1 Basic standard cost diagram.

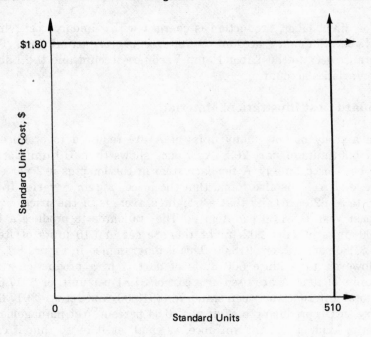

Figure 8.2 Comparison of standard and actual costs.

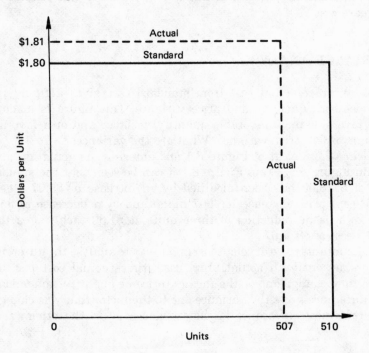

Figure 8.3 Computing variance on the basis of quantity first.

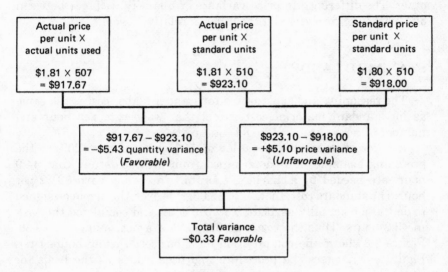

Figure 8.4 Computing variance on the basis of price first.

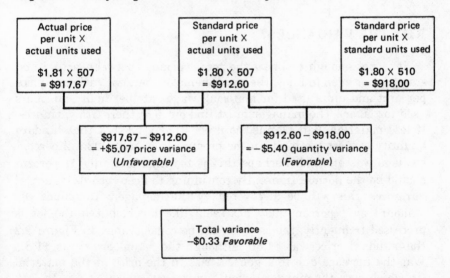

In Figure 8.3 the quantity factor is first changed. In Figure 8.4, the alternate factor (that is, the price) is changed first. If actual cost is less than standard cost, the net variance is favorable; if not, the net variance is unfavorable.

Note in Figure 8.4 the slight difference in the analysis of Figure

8.3, which occurs because one of the factors was changed before the other. The difference in price variance or quantity variance between one method of analysis and the other is relatively small.

STANDARD LABOR

The reasoning and explanation for standard labor cost is the same as for standard material cost except that wage rate per hour and number of hours are used to get total costs.

Assume that to produce a lot of 500 units of part 202 in the preceding example, it is determined from previous study that 44.9 hours are needed by a machine operator who would earn $3.52 per hour. The standard cost, then, is $158.05. However, the person assigned to do the job actually earned $3.60 per hour, and completed the task in 43.2 hours. Thus the cost was $155.52, or a net savings of $2.53. Figure 8.5 shows the computation for labor costs, using hours first. Figure 8.6 reverses the procedure and uses wages as the basis for analysis.

WHY THE VARIANCES?

It is not enough to know the total variance between actual and standard, or even to know the components of the total variance (price per unit and units used for material; wage rate per hour and hours used for labor). The manager must find out *why* there are variances. If less material than planned is used, it may be that the standard quantity was set too high. In the production of part 202 a 2 percent spoilage was allowed. Perhaps this is too high and only $1\frac{1}{2}$ percent should be the normal figure. By continuing to keep records on actual variances, this will be discovered by the manager. To reduce the standard by $\frac{1}{2}$ percent may not seem like much, but if the lot is processed frequently, the savings can be considerable. In Figure 8.2 the standard price was $1.80, although the actual price was $1.81. Was the increase due to a general rise in the price of the material (in which case the standard should be raised) or was it due to lack of care in purchasing (in which case, perhaps, the purchasing procedures should be tightened to secure better prices)? These queries will also be asked by the manager. For standard labor costs (Figure 8.5), the questions asked might be:

Figure 8.5 Computing variance on the basis of hours first.

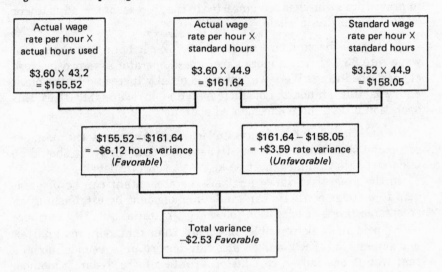

Figure 8.6 Computing variance on the basis of wages first.

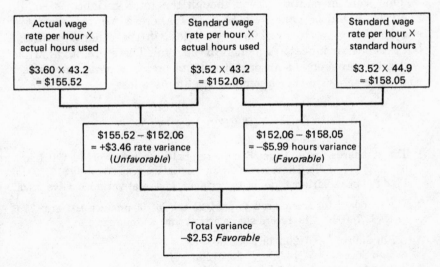

1. Is the standard-hour period of 44.9 hours realistic when only 43.2 actual hours were needed to complete the job? Perhaps that particular operator is a better-than-average worker. But it is also possible that the standards were set some time ago and that an improved procedure has been inserted in the process, but no adjustment of the time has been made.

2. Why is the standard wage rate $3.52 per hour, but the actual wage rate $3.60? Was a more experienced operator assigned because of poor scheduling? Were wage rates generally increased in the plant and was this standard not increased due to oversight? Does this operation need a more experienced operator?

By questioning the variances and looking for answers, the manager can make the operation more efficient and less costly. It should be understood that quality must be kept at a constant level.

In the area of variance analysis the accountant can be of great help to management. He can guide management by establishing an acceptable range of exception tolerances (material quantity variance of ±1 percent is permissible, but more than that requires analysis and action; etc.). The manager also can convert an "eyeshade" accountant who is basically a cost historian into a more dynamic member of the management team.

One word of caution: Even though the total variance is small, analyses should be done. It may be that there is a large saving in one dimension with an almost equal loss in the other dimension, but that the variances are hidden in the total. Therefore, an analysis will give management an opportunity to protect savings and effect corrective action to cut or completely eliminate loss.

QUESTIONS

1. The standards for material B used to produce a lot of product 101 are: 650 lb @ $17.15/lb. The record shows an actual usage of 665 lb @ $17.10/lb. Find the price variance, quantity variance, and total variance. Give proof.

2. The standard for labor used to produce the lot of product 101 are: 72.6 hr @ $3.760/hr. The record shows actual time as follows:

Bill Smith	20.2 hr @ $3.50/hr
Sam Spade	14.3 hr @ $3.75/hr
John Jackson	22.7 hr @ $3.80/hr
Walt Harold	15.8 hr @ $3.85/hr

Find the labor rate variance, hours variance, and total variance.

9

Budgets

BUDGETING is the key to financial control. In other areas the process might be called model building. Both terms connote the same objective—the simulation of operating results, given certain conditions. It isn't enough to decide what to do. The decision maker should have some idea of the consequences of his decisions so that he can tailor them to his particular area of interest.

Proper budgeting requires thought and care. It involves a number of things indirectly related to finance, such as corporate purpose, organizational structure, communications, reporting, and corrective action-taking. It may involve short- and long-range corporate plans. It certainly requires a study of the company's operations.

COMPANY STUDY

Goals. In a company study the goals of the company should be stated clearly. "Our company wants to produce a superior product" does not necessarily equate to "Our company's share of the market must be 30 percent or more." In too many cases the goals are not written down, are not clearly understood by top management, and are relatively unknown at the lower levels of management.

Organization chart. Once the goals are stated, management must devise an organization to achieve those goals. In an ongoing business the organization chart helps identify positions and their relationships. Often, however, the organization chart tends to show the organization as someone would like it to be, rather than what it is. Another criticism is that an organization chart, once prepared, tends to stifle organizational reshuffling as needed, or if it is reshuffled does not result in a new chart because of the time, effort, and expense involved.

Position descriptions. It is imperative that management assign to each individual in the organization a set of tasks. The preparation by individuals of a job description covering their position will reveal to management what the individual perceives his job to be. However, management's review of these job interpretations will find some employees doing too much or too little, some tasks performed by more than one individual, and other necessary tasks done by no one. Using these preliminary job studies, management can reassign tasks to keep work loads equitably distributed, see that each task is assigned to only one individual, and make sure that all necessary tasks are assigned. After these adjustments are made, official job descriptions should be written, filed in a binder, and communicated in writing to the position incumbent.

When all this is done, the organizational framework is structured for budgeting.

OPERATIONAL FRAMEWORK

Once the accounting department has a logical organizational structure, it can proceed to assign costs. It should develop a series of accounts by number, each of which corresponds to a selected business area. These account numbers will be used for budget preparation, accounting data collection, and reporting of operational results.

The accounting department should prepare an accounting manual of definitions, describing what goes into each category so that the budget data will be developed in the same manner in which accounting data are collected. Copies of this manual should be distributed to the persons responsible for budget preparation. Budgets are best prepared by lower-level line supervisors for costs they control. These budgets are then moved upward through the organization. At each level the data are reviewed (and discussed with the preparer, when necessary) and consolidated, and finally an overall company budget is presented to the Board of Directors or other appropriate body for approval.

Types of Budget

Budgets may cover either a short-range (one year) or long-range (three to five years or longer) period. Some companies use both. The short-range budget will be more detailed by department or group and type of expense in each; the long-range will be less specific and not overly detailed as to type of expense.

The short-range budget may be prepared for one year and remain fixed for that period. This is called the "Yearly Budget." Another approach is to prepare a budget for some future year, but to revise it quarterly to add new data, and then extend it for another year. This is called the "rolling" or "dynamic" budget, and is considered preferable. Figure 9.1 compares the two budget plans.

Figure 9.1 Comparison of yearly and rolling budgets.

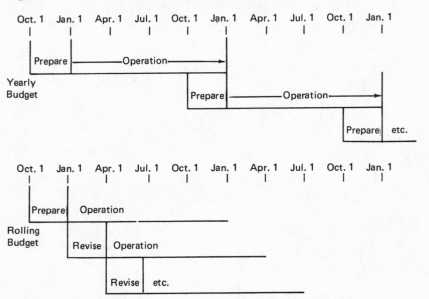

It can be readily seen that in a rolling budget the operator has updated figures for 12 months operation at least 9 months in advance. Changes in sales and production volumes, material prices, wage rates, organizational structure, competition, economic conditions, etc., can be adjusted by the budget preparation process to produce a forecast that more closely resembles the real environment on an ongoing basis.

Static versus flexible budgets. Budgets may be prepared for one level of activity (static budget), or for a number of levels of activity (flexible budget). The better of the two budgets, in the author's opinion, is the flexible budget. This type requires a greater knowledge of cost behavior, implying that a more detailed study of costs has been made. More importantly, however, when the final operating results are in, it is a rather simple task to interpolate actual costs between two of the options where real volume falls. Then a comparison can be better made on a dispassionate basis—and probably a more accurate comparison will be made because it is less likely that there will be a "bending" of the figures to make actual performance look better than it really is.

A *better budget*. Perhaps the best of all systems to use is a flexible rolling budget. This costs money, but in the long run the savings should far outweigh the costs.

10

Analysis of Factory Overhead Variance

In the Chapter 6 discussion of factory overhead, it was mentioned that factory costs and appropriate distribution units were estimated. In Chapter 9 on the subject of budgets, the idea of levels of activities was mentioned with regard to the flexible budget.

What are the premises on which the cost of an activity in a company is determined? First is the level of production, perhaps expressed as *capacity* in percentage terms. Second is the price per unit of economic utility purchased, and the formulation of this cost may vary, depending on the particular utility purchased (from fixed to variable in any manner, as discussed in Chapter 7). Third is some notion of corporate efficiency; that is, the amount of utility used to produce a stated value of product.

This can be illustrated by a three-dimensional model. Suppose that the corner of a room is used to simulate this model. If the corner defined by the two walls is the *price-per-unit* axis, then the cost-per-unit of whatever utility we were discussing could be marked by a point on the vertical line formed by the walls. On the line formed by one of the walls and the floor, we would define *capacity*, with the "normal" capacity marked on that line. On the line formed by the other wall and the floor, we would define *efficiency*, with the "normal" efficiency marked on that line. If, then, a plane were passed through these three points, it would enclose a given volume. This volume would represent the budget for that utility—given a price per unit of utility, a "normal" capacity, and a "normal" efficiency. If all these conditions were met exactly, then the actual dollar expenditure for this utility would be exactly equal to the budgeted estimate of its cost.

In the operating world, however, there is a high probability that these three conditions would not be met exactly. There would then be a variance in dollars between the actual and budgeted figures. Figure 10.1 illustrates the relationship of these three factors and how the movement of each one affects total expenditure.

In giving direction to the three lines in Figure 10.1, an upward movement in cost per utility unit would increase the total expenditure; a downward movement, decrease it. A decrease in capacity (production) would decrease the total expenditure; an increase in capacity, increase

Figure 10.1 Determining cost of company activity.

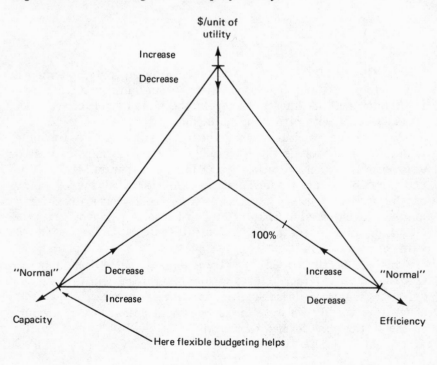

it. An increase in efficiency would decrease total expenditure; a decrease in efficiency, increase it. (Note: There is still an expenditure even if the company achieves 100 percent efficiency.)

With flexible budgeting in effect a series of planes are developed and it would be relatively simple to interpolate total expenditure between two *different production levels.* This is based on the assumption that costs will probably vary linearly between two levels, if the levels are not too far apart. Where this assumption does not hold true, the previous study (Chapter 7) of cost behavior would give the desired data at the actual level.

The *price/utility unit difference* can be measured between the rates set by vendors on actual invoices and the rates used in the budget process. Any material change in rate can also be used to change cash requirements if cash forecasts are made.

The *efficiency dimension* is harder to measure. Probably the easiest solution would be to take the remaining variance difference and call it the efficiency variance. However, if statistical data have been developed sufficiently to derive a particular amount of an economic utility that would normally be used at specific production levels, then a variance in the amount used would be a true measure of efficiency variance. For example: Assume that flexible budgeting is used for 10,000 unit levels from 100,000 to 150,000. The price per utility unit is $1.10 per unit. It has been anticipated that production will be 120,000 at $9,460. Table 10.1 shows usage of the utility unit and its cost at the various unit levels under "normal" efficiency.

is $1.10 per unit. It has been anticipated that production will be 120,000 at $9,460. Table 10.1 shows usage of the utility unit and its cost at the various unit levels under "normal" efficiency.

Table 10.1

Units	Utility Units	Cost @ $1.10/ Utility Unit
100,000	7,000	$ 7,700
110,000	7,900	8,690
120,000	8,600	9,460
130,000	9,400	10,340
140,000	10,100	11,110
150,000	10,900	11,990

Actual production is 134,000 units (see Table 10.2), the utility units used are 9,850, and the cost/utility unit price is $1.08 for a

Table 10.2

Budget at 120,000 units	$ 9,460	
Budget at 134,000 units	10,648	
Budget variance (*unfavorable*)	$ 1,188	
Price/unit @ $1.10 for 9,850 units	$10,835	
Price/unit @ $1.08 for 9,850 units	10,638	
Price variance (*favorable*)	$ 197	
Units at "normal" efficiency:		
[(10,100 − 9,400) × (4/10)] + 9,400	9,680	
Units at actual efficiency	9,850	
Excess units (*unfavorable*)	170	
Excess units @ $1.10	$ 187	
Budget variance	$ 1,188	unfavorable
Price/unit variance	197	favorable
Efficiency variance	187	unfavorable
Total variance	$ 1,178	unfavorable

Proof		
Budget at 120,000 units	$ 9,460	
Actual costs	10,638	
Total variance	$ 1,178	

total cost of $10,638. The total variance is $1,178 unfavorable. The budgeted cost is $10,648 ([($11,110 − $10,340) × (4/10)] + $10,340).

QUESTIONS

1. The budget is planned for 240,000 units and the cost for a particular utility is budgeted for $172,000. A flexible budget shows the following: for 250,000 units, $180,000; 260,000 units, $189,000. The production was actually 256,000 units. What is the budget variance?

2. The price per unit of utility used in the budget was $5.00 per unit of utility for a planned production of 70,000 units. Actually, 77,000 units were produced and 8,300 units of utility were used at $5.10 per unit. What is the price variance?

3. The following data were developed from the records of REMCO: Production is scheduled for 82,000 units. The budgeted cost for an overhead item is 4,700 units @ $6.50 per unit. The analysis used to develop these figures shows the following price behavior for this item:

Production	Units Used
70,000	3,750
80,000	4,500
90,000	5,500

Actually, 79,000 units were produced. The usage of this item was 4,400 units and the cost was $6.60 per unit.

Compute (a) budget variance; (b) price variance; (c) efficiency variance; (d) total variance for this item.

11

Cost Principles Applied to Selling and Administrative Expenses

TRADITIONALLY, cost accounting was applied to the area of industry that was producing goods. In the production area there was physical movement and changes in goods that could be readily seen. It was always necessary to determine costs per unit for purposes of determining sales prices and gross profit margins. The sales and administrative areas were treated as a "service" as long as the total expenses were reasonable (that is, a tolerable percentage of sales or at least such that the profit was within acceptable limits). No serious effort was made to study costs in these areas of the business.

When industry began to realize that there is a production sequence going on in the service areas, although this production per se is not sold, then studies relating to total costs, total output, cost per unit of output, and increase in efficiency became more common.

THE SALES AREA

What are the "units of production" in sales? How about number of customers seen, number of orders prepared, number of phone calls made, etc.? Having such data available, management might find that total sales expense is reasonable, but on further analysis it also might find that the number of customers seen by each salesman ranges from 8 to 30 per week, with a median of 20. Now management has some data to use in its study of individual effort. Why the large range? If all salesmen are paid a flat salary, or a salary varying according to years of service, might commissions be a better method of payment? Are there territorial differences that might account for the range? What can be done to reduce the cost per dollar of sales?

These questions may not be immediately answerable because there may be no data presently available. There may not even be a simple way of getting the data. Therefore, a revision of the data collection system may be necessary. The Sales Journal may need to be expanded to include the name of the salesman so that, in addition to total sales, a report can be prepared showing sales by each salesman. Perhaps the Sales Journal should be further expanded to analyze sales by type of product. Then an additional report can be prepared showing sales by salesman and product. By using computers, input data can be expanded so that the analysis, cross-analysis, and subanalysis of data can be developed to inform management. Management can then apply corrective action in the particular subset of costs where efficiency is below the level desired. Management might also study the better-than-average performances to see if there is something in the sales approach used that can be applied to the below-level performance areas.

When these corrective actions are applied, it may be discovered that total sales costs have not declined but that total sales have increased. This, however, will increase profitability, as the accompanying table shows.

	Before Analysis	After Analysis
Sales	$1,000,000 (100%)	$1,100,000 (100%)
Cost of sales	800,000 (80%)	880,000 (80%)
	200,000 (20%)	220,000 (20%)
Sales expense	120,000 (12%)	120,000 (11%)
Profit*	$ 80,000 (8%)	$ 100,000 (9%)

*Administrative expenses are not considered here and percentages are rounded.

A study of sales effort and the application of some corrective action has increased the profit by $20,000, and assuming that this study cost less than that, there is a net increase in profit. (One must not lose sight of the fact that the study is made once, but the cost savings might well be realized year after year.) At the old percentage rates, sales would have to be increased by $250,000 to yield an additional $20,000 in profit. It is evident that it is preferable to use the present sales staff more efficiently than it is to increase the staff to get the 25% increase in sales *plus* the added sales expense *in sales* to produce the extra $20,000 in profit.

THE ADMINISTRATIVE AREA

What about "production units" in the administrative area? Some that might be used are letters written, files pulled, letters (or catalogs, etc.) mailed, and so forth. Here again there may be a dearth of data, but once management begins to think in terms of measuring output, the data can be developed. Again ranges in performance will begin to develop, and the better and poorer producers can be identified. Many office equipment suppliers have accumulated data that will give management a place to start in its measurement of output. With repetitive tasks, data can be more readily generated internally or secured from industry studies.

With nonrepetitive tasks, data are more difficult to secure, but can still be developed to discover good and poor performance. It needs only some imagination to develop a reporting format that will give significant data to management so that it can better control the use of resources.

Two large problems loom in the effective use of data in the nonrepetitive area. The first is the way to persuade personnel to turn in the data and to report it honestly. This may require time sheets that must be turned in on a regular schedule, and some testing to insure that the data turned in are valid. The second is the method of analyzing the data in some meaningful fashion so that management can take corrective action. It is the author's belief that in the higher echelons of the enterprise, some resistance will be encountered, but the task is not insurmountable. In many accounting firms and legal firms, for example, staff time sheets are required for billing purposes, and senior partners as well as staff personnel turn these in. Therefore, it is imperative to explain to officers of the company the reasons for collecting these data and to secure their approval. It is well to ask for their cooperation and to point out that they will set an example for employees by preparing and turning in their own time sheets.

12

Management Control Reports

WHAT the accountant develops in the course of his work must be communicated to management. Frequently this information is presented in forms that accountants understand but not in a way that the nonaccountant can grasp and use. Perhaps some clarification of the very words in the title of the chapter will be useful: The accountant must send to management *reports* that contain visual presentations of data so that *management* can use the data to *control* the changes in the economic behavior of the firm. Management control reports should be simple and concise but more explanatory than the formal statements that are prepared for stockholders, creditors, or outsiders.

FORMAT

What should management demand of the data preparers? Since the purpose of the data is to aid in control, there is an implication that management knows where it wants the firm to go. But this must be formulated and communicated to all levels of the organization so that in policy matters everyone is going the same way. Some reports will be expository, others in accounting format, and others in graphic display.

Expository reports. These may be all or any of the following:
1. A clear statement of company philosophy, or of goals and aims.
2. A job-description manual containing details of the duties and responsibilities for each position.
3. A budget-preparation manual outlining the chronology of budget preparation, and defining participation and coordination levels.
4. A chart of accounts with explanations of account content and expense object description.

Accounting format. Reports of this type include:
1. The budget.
2. Monthly departmental reports.
3. Variance reports.
4. Other numerically expressed data such as number of direct labor hours, units sold, wage scales.

Graphic displays. Various graphic presentations include:
1. Charts.
2. Semilog charts.
3. Pie charts.
4. Bar charts.
5. Overlays that update statistics on existing charts, etc.
6. Relational diagrams (like the organizational chart).

Since management is going to use the information, it should be prepared in the form that the manager is used to working with. Therefore the accountant may be required, when he communicates data to management, to present that data in a "not accounting" format.

REPORTING LEVELS

Accounting data for the whole firm, in whatever format presented, can consist of a large volume of material. The accountant may submit the material in a single document to be sent to all responsibility control centers, or he may send each center only those documents pertinent to its control. Whichever he chooses is his prerogative, but in the author's opinion, the accountant should prepare a complete set of data and then select subsets of those data and send them to responsibility cost centers to assist in control.

Each person who heads a responsibility cost center should get data about his immediate subordinates, about the peers in his functional area, and about the information given to his superior. The purpose of having data about his immediate subordinates is that this group is his responsibility for control purposes, and he needs to know what data affect it. The reason for having data about the peers in his functional area is that he can use the information to compare the performance of his group against other like groups. The reason for having the data given to his superior is that he can know (and verify) what the center head sees as his share of the total effort of which he is a part.

For example, A is a divisional sales manager responsible for a territory that has three salesmen (S1, S2, and S3). He reports to regional sales manager 1, who has three divisional sales managers (A, B, C) reporting to him. Figure 12.1 is a diagram of the organization

Figure 12.1

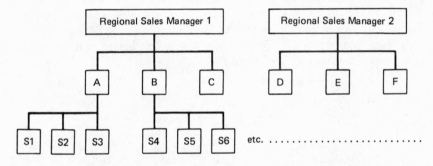

hierarchy and corresponding flow of reports from the respective cost centers. One report to A consists of the details and summaries of the efforts, costs, and results of S1, S2, and S3. He would not get data on S4, S5, S6, etc. Another report to A would be the summaries of the efforts, costs, and results of B and C. He would not get data on D, E, or F. Another report to A would be pertinent data about A given to regional sales manager 1, but nothing given to regional sales manager 2.

REPORT TIMING

To be useful for control purposes, reports should be issued on a regular basis soon after the close of the reporting period. This period may be monthly or quarterly, which is the traditional accounting interval timing, but may be weekly, biweekly, or some other time period that is appropriate to control.

Not all reports need have the same time period. Sales reports may be weekly, whereas production reports may be semimonthly. The frequency should be dictated by the user's need for information that affects control.

In order to get the information out as soon as possible after the period ends (three to five days may well be the time), there may be some estimates of data for the last few days of the period. This means that "cents" accuracy may be sacrificed to secure report timeliness; that seems to be a fair trade-off.

ACTION ORIENTATION

The reports that compare expected and actual performance should point out to the manager those items that he must do something about or should be watching, or which are acceptable at present. The presentation should separate controllable costs (shown at the top) from uncontrollable costs (shown at the bottom). Let us examine a sales performance report (Table 12.1).

Table 12.1

| | Monthly | | | | Year to Date | | | |
	Budget Dollars	Actual Dollars	Variance $M	%	Budget Dollars	Actual Dollars	Variance $M	%
Sales A	40,000	41,000	1	2.5	127,000	129,000	2	1.6
Sales B	70,000	75,000	5	7.1	220,000	222,000	2	0.9
Sales C	90,000	89,000	(1)	(1.1)	277,000	278,000	1	0.4
Sales D	80,000	75,000	(5)	(6.3)	235,000	243,000	8	3.4
Total	280,000	280,000	0	0	859,000	872,000	13	1.5

Perhaps after establishing a tolerance range for an item, any figure outside that range would be subject to action, and any figures close to the outer limits of the range would be watched. If the range for monthly sales were ±5 percent, then Sales B and Sales D would require action. If the tolerance for year to date were ±3 percent, only Sales D would require action. Why action on those items that exceed the expected? So that the performance can be reviewed to see why there was a better than expected performance, and to give the ideas that produced that superior performance to others in the company who are performing the same tasks so that their efficiencies can be increased. The manager may also want to review the performance of Sales C, since the negative performance shown by the monthly figure is eroding the previous positive performance of C.

Let us now examine an expense report.

	Budget Dollars	Actual Dollars	Variance $	%
Utilities	10,000	9,700	(300)	(3.0)
Telephone	14,000	14,700	700	5.0

Note that what is being compared is actual to budget and is *not* the effects on profits. The negative $300 variance *increases* profits; the positive $700 variance *decreases* profits. The manager wants all expenses variances on the negative side.

OTHER FORMATS

The accountant should become familiar with and use nonaccounting formats.

Charts

The chart is the familiar line or curve form used for presenting data. It consists of two axes at right angles to each other—one reading upward (the ordinate) on the vertical scale (see Figure 12.2); the

Figure 12.2

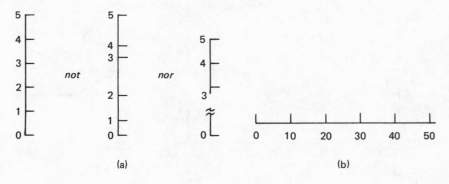

(a)   (b)

other to the right on the horizontal scale (the abscissa). The increments of unit values on a scale should be equal in length. The scales should be clearly labeled. There should be no break in the scale continuum because data may be distorted. The chart should be clearly labeled to state what it purports to show.

If the purpose of the chart is to show two or more items and how they are valued over time, it is best to use the horizontal axes for both so that the relative movement of one is not confused by the relative movement of the other. When cumulative data are to be shown and the individual data groups are pertinent, perhaps two charts may show this better. Figures 12.3 and 12.4 illustrate these principles. The chart in Figure 12.3 shows the line for A, and above

Figure 12.3

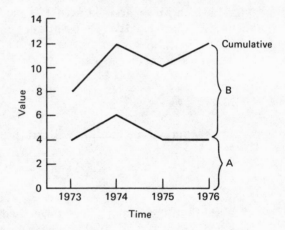

Figure 12.4

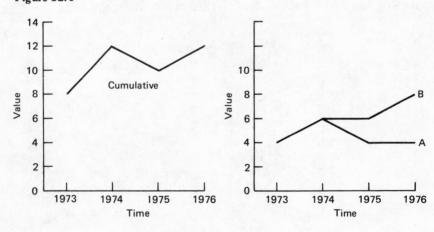

it the line for B, which becomes the cumulative of the two. Now if we look at Figure 12.4, in which the cumulative is shown as a separate chart, we can see from the second chart that B (measured from the horizontal axis) was never less than it was the year before, and that A was responsible for the dip in the cumulative curve. However, that is not readily apparent in Figure 12.3.

When two or more lines are shown on one chart, it may well be worthwhile to use different colored lines or different styled lines to distinguish between components.

Charts are easy to prepare if the accountant uses preprinted forms with wax rub-off lines; these can be purchased in many art supply stores.

One chart that could be prepared for control use might be made by plotting the budgeted and actual figures so that the variance may be seen directly.

Semilog Charts

The use of semilog paper in preparing charts is very effective because its characteristic makes trend analysis data readily apparent. Semilog paper is laid out with even increments on the horizontal axis, but the vertical axis is laid out in increments like those on a slide rule.

Let us assume that the data for four years of sales are: 1973, $100,000; 1974, $150,000; and 1975, $180,000. The chart is shown in Figure 12.5. From year 1973 to 1974 sales increased 50 percent. Any two points connected by a line with the same slope as that between 100 and 150 will also have gone up 50 percent. In Figure 12.6, five parallel lines are plotted between 1973 and 1974, and the values are shown at each end of the lines. All are 50 percent greater in 1974 than in 1973. Note also in Figure 12.5 that the slope of the line between 1974 and 1975 is flatter than the rise between 1973 and 1974. This happens because the percentage rise between 1974 and 1975 was less (20%) than the year before. The slope, then, tells the relative change from one period to another.

Pie Chart

The pie chart is often used to present data. Basically, it is a circle radially divided so that the area in each space is proportional to the percentage of the whole that each group of data represents. For example, let Figure 12.7 show the sales data in Table 12.2. To obtain

Figure 12.5

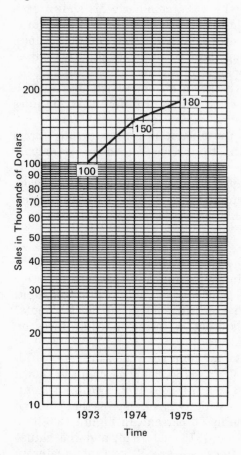

Figure 12.6

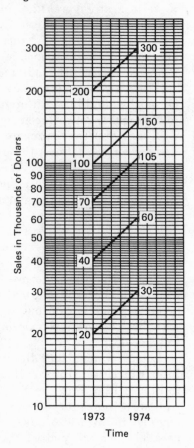

Figure 12.7

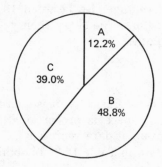

Figure 12.8

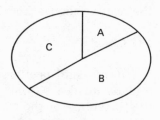

Table 12.2

	Dollar Sales	Percentage	Angle,°
Item A	10,000	12.2	44
Item B	40,000	48.8	176
Item C	32,000	39.0	140
Total	82,000	100.0	360

the area in the circle for each component, multiply the total 360 degrees of the circle by the percentage of sales for each item. Each of the segments on the circumference of the circle will be proportional to the percentage of sales for items A, B, and C.

Sometimes the circle is tilted and becomes an ellipse, but this distorts the data presentation. In Figure 12.8 the same data presented in Figure 12.7 are tilted 60 percent from the circular position; therefore the proportional division is not accurate.

When comparing two items in pie-chart form (for example, income and expense for an enterprise) make both pie charts the same size and show the difference (either an income or a deficit) on the appropriate chart, as in Figure 12.9. This is sound from an accounting standpoint and is also more understandable to the reader.

Figure 12.9

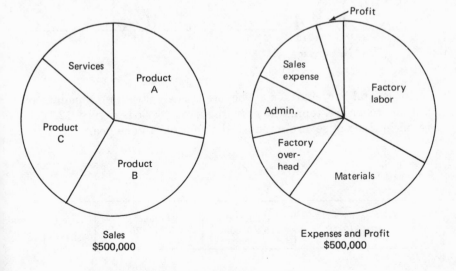

Sales
$500,000

Expenses and Profit
$500,000

Bar Charts

Another way to present data is by means of bar charts. A bar chart consists of a rectangular space that may be measured off vertically or horizontally to show magnitude. The vertical-bar type is used to graph amounts of a variable at different time intervals.

One form of bar chart uses one length to show one item of data and another proportionate length to show another item of data. For example, to compare the sales of two years, the chart may appear with vertical bars as in Figure 12.10, which shows that in 1975, sales were $300,000; 1976, $400,000.

It is preferable to leave space between bars. Overlapping, as in Figure 12.11, is confusing, if not actually misleading, because the overlaps may be interpreted as a two-year span instead of spans for individual years.

Figure 12.10   **Figure 12.11**

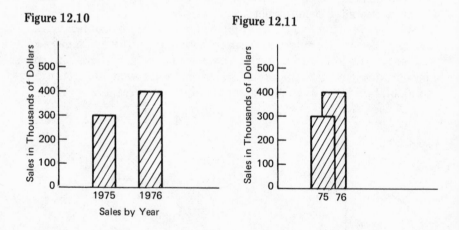

Horizontal-bar charts may be used when different amounts of several items are represented in the same period. Figure 12.12 is a typical chart of several product distributions in one year.

Figure 12.12

Product A 32% $128M	Product B 25% $100M	Product C 30% $120M	Other 13% $52M

Another version of the bar chart is the 100 percent type, in which the vertical bars are divided into sections representing different items. For example, in Figure 12.13 the percentage of sales for each product (see Figure 12.12) A, B, C is linked with the succeeding year's data for easy comparison of product activity. Without the dashed lead lines in Figure 12.13, it would be harder to see the changes in product sales because the base lines have shifted in 1975.

Figure 12.13

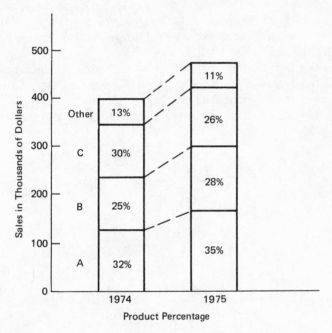

Product Percentage

Overlays

The use of color, shading, or other distinguishing markings may also affect how the viewer sees a display. In some cases where presentations are made by the accountant, he may be building up a concept from some basic idea and want to add to it in the development of the presentation. Here, overlays may prove beneficial. The basic idea is to put the basic data on an opaque medium and put additions on a transparent medium that can be placed over the original whenever the presentation requires new material. Transparencies are usually superposed one at a time, but more could be used as long as the viewer can see through them. In this way a complete idea can be presented visually in stages so that the viewer will not be confused by added items until they have been explained and presented.

CREATIVITY AND IMAGINATION

The examples and illustrations in this chapter should give the reader an idea as to how data may be prepared and presented. Any serious student of the subject will want to get more information on graphics for use in business. The nonaccounting manager should feel free to ask the accountant to present data in a format that is familiar and therefore more readily usable by him.

Once the accountant sees that there is a positive reaction to new ways of data presentation, he may then be encouraged to explore new techniques. He will exercise his creativity and imagination in developing better and better possibilities for clearer and more concise statements.

APPENDIX A

The Certificate in Management Accounting

THE traditional role of the accountant in private industry has been that of a recorder of business history. As business became larger, as government regulation became more extensive and tax consequences of business transactions became more acute, the accountant's role has evolved into a closer partnership with management at the decision-making level. Over recent years an informal designation of "management accountant" has been used to describe this role. The accountant's function has become one of developing, producing, and analyzing data to help management make better decisions.

The National Association of Accountants recognized the changing nature of the accountant's functions when it renamed its monthly publication *Management Accounting* in 1957. NAA led other professional accounting organizations in establishing the Institute of Management Accounting, to administer the Certificate in Management Accounting program. The program's primary objectives are to:

1. Establish management accounting as a profession.
2. Foster higher educational standards in the profession.
3. Establish an objective measure of an individual's knowledge and competence in the profession.

The Institute of Management Accounting has instituted a program of examinations to measure the accountant's knowledge. At present, these examinations are given once a year in June over a period of two and one-half days, and cover the following subject areas:

1. Economics and Business Finance
2. Organization and Behavior, including Ethical Considerations
3. Public Reporting Standards, Auditing, and Taxes
4. Periodic Reporting for Internal and External Purposes
5. Decision Analysis, including Modeling and Information Systems

IMA evaluates accounting knowledge and requires two years of professional experience. Upon completion of these two requirements the Certificate in Management Accounting (CMA) designation is given to the accountant. To date, the Institute has granted 385 CMAs.

For further information write to:

Institute of Management Accounting
570 City Center Building
Ann Arbor, Michigan 48104

APPENDIX B

Selected Courses
for More Information

American Management Associations
135 W. 50th Street
New York, New York 10020

The American Management Associations has for over 50 years been concerned with bettering management performance. It sponsors a wide variety of educational opportunities for the individuals who want to improve their managerial skills. One of the methods it uses effectively is the Meetings Program. These meetings are held in various key cities in the United States and in foreign countries. The meetings run from $2\frac{1}{2}$ to 5 days.

Course Number	Title
1201	Fundamentals of Cost Accounting
1210	Inventory Costing
1256	Flexible Budgeting
1284	Profitability Accounting and Control
1320	Inflation Accounting

1517–8	Fundamentals of Finance and Accounting for Non-Financial Executives
1526	Fundamentals of Budgeting
3284	Communicating Employee Benefits
3511	Fundamentals of Employee Benefits
4206	Inventory Management and Control
4252	Fundamentals of Industrial Engineering
4263	Manufacturing Cost Estimating
4271	Fundamentals of Manufacturing Management for Newly Appointed Manufacturing Line Supervisors
4501	Production Planning and Control
8521	Job Evaluation and Wage Salary Administration
11251	Fundamentals of Management for Warehouse Managers
11501	Purchasing Management
12154	Establishing and Controlling Corporate Manuals
12258	Preparing Administrative Manuals

Continuing Education Units (CEUs) are given for these courses.

National Association of Accountants
919 Third Avenue
New York, New York 10022

The National Association of Accountants has for over 50 years been concerned with fostering professionalism among cost (now called "management") accountants. It publishes the monthly *Management Accounting*, and in recent years has sponsored a Continuing Education Program (CEP) and other programs. The following CEP programs run 2 or 3 days:

Developing and Using Standard Costs
Flexible Budgeting and Performance Reporting
Direct Costing and Contribution Accounting
Management Accounting for Executives and Managers
Accounting Information for Pricing
Inventory Management and Control
Management Science for Budgeting and Profit Planning

American Institute of Certified Public Accountants
1211 Avenue of the Americas
New York, New York 10036

The AICPA coordinates its activities with the state societies of

CPAs in the various states. CPAs in many states are required to secure continuing education credit as a requirement for license renewal. The AICPA and the state societies have developed many courses especially for accountants. Some of these courses relate to the cost accounting area. The distribution of course data is limited to CPAs who are members of AICPA and/or the state societies, but is also available to Public Accountants. The auditor of the reader's firm or his personal accountant may be willing to arrange attendance at these meetings for him.

Many local colleges and universities also have regular undergraduate and graduate classes as well as special seminars (or noncredit courses given for the nondegree student) at hours convenient for those who are employed.

APPENDIX C

The Cost Accounting Standards Board

THE Cost Accounting Standards Board (CASB) was created as an agent of the Congress in 1970 and was formally organized in 1971.

The CASB is charged with developing cost accounting standards for increased uniformity and consistency in cost accounting practices of contractors dealing with the federal government. The CASB isolates an area or topic for study and reviews the accounting concepts involved through an examination of the accounting literature and meetings with representatives of professional accounting organizations (the American Accounting Association; the American Institute of Certified Public Accountants; the Association of Government Accountants; the Financial Executives Institute; and the National Association of Accountants), members of CPA firms, university faculty members, and other interested parties.

It assesses alternative accounting procedures and prepares a preliminary draft of a standard. This preliminary draft may be circulated to interested parties for review and comment. When all data are in, the whole procedure for the proposed standard is reviewed. If a decision is made to proceed, the revised proposed standard is published in the *Federal Register* for wider exposure, review, and comment. Comments are evaluated and the proposed standard is again revised and published in the *Federal Register*, with annotations of changes in the text. At the same time, the proposed standard is sent to Congress, which can pass a resolution stating that it does not favor the standard. The CASB is also charged with the continuing responsibility of evaluating the effectiveness of the materials it promulgates.

Since its inception, the CASB has issued eleven cost accounting standards on the following subjects:

1. Consistency in Estimating, Accumulating, and Reporting Costs
2. Consistency in Allocating Costs Incurred for the Same Purpose
3. Allocation of Home Office Costs to Segments
4. Capitalization of Tangible Assets
5. Accounting for Unallowable Costs
6. Cost Accounting Period
7. Use of Standard Cost for Direct Material and Direct Labor
8. Accounting for Costs of Compensated Personal Absence
9. Depreciation of Tangible Capital Assets
10. Accounting for Acquisition of Materials
11. Composition and Measurement of Pension Costs

There are at present 17 studies at various stages of the procedure, and these may very well develop into standards. These studies are concerned with general and administrative expense allocation to final cost objects; cost of capital; manufacturing, overhead allocation; costs of contract direct materials not incorporated in the end product; costs of service centers; contract termination accounting; deferred compensation; indirect costs of colleges and universities; distinguishing between direct and indirect costs; independent R & D and bid and proposal costs; insurance cost accounting; intracompany transfer accounting; adjustment and association of pension costs; material related expenses; engineering overhead; other operations overhead; and terminology.

As can be seen from the list of cost accounting standards that have been promulgated and from the far-ranging research topics being investigated, the CASB has had and will continue to have a profound effect on cost accounting.

APPENDIX D   Table 1   Present value of $1.00 due at the end of N years.

$$S = \frac{x}{(1 + i)^N}$$

N	1%	2%	3%	4%	5%	6%	7%	8%	9%	10%	N
01	0.99010	0.98039	0.97007	0.96154	0.95238	0.94340	0.93458	0.92593	0.91743	0.90909	01
02	.98030	.96117	.94260	.92456	.90703	.89000	.87344	.85734	.84168	.82645	02
03	.97059	.94232	.91514	.88900	.86384	.83962	.81630	.79383	.77218	.75131	03
04	.96098	.92385	.88849	.85480	.82270	.79209	.76290	.73503	.70843	.68301	04
05	.95147	.90573	.86261	.82193	.78353	.74726	.71299	.68058	.64993	.62092	05
06	.94204	.88797	.83748	.79031	.74622	.70496	.66634	.63017	.59627	.56447	06
07	.93272	.87056	.81309	.75992	.71068	.66506	.62275	.58349	.54703	.51316	07
08	.92348	.85349	.78941	.73069	.67684	.62741	.58201	.54027	.50187	.46651	08
09	.91434	.83675	.76642	.70259	.64461	.59190	.54393	.50025	.46043	.42410	09
10	.90529	.82035	.74409	.67556	.61391	.55839	.50835	.46319	.42241	.38554	10
11	.89632	.80426	.72242	.64958	.58468	.52679	.47509	.42888	.38753	.35049	11
12	.88745	.78849	.70138	.62460	.55684	.49697	.44401	.39711	.35553	.31863	12
13	.87866	.77303	.68095	.60057	.53032	.46884	.41496	.36770	.32618	.28966	13
14	.86996	.75787	.66112	.57747	.50507	.44230	.38782	.34046	.29925	.26333	14
15	.86135	.74301	.64186	.55526	.48102	.41726	.36245	.31524	.27454	.23939	15
16	.85282	.72845	.62317	.53391	.45811	.39365	.33873	.29189	.25187	.21763	16
17	.84438	.71416	.60502	.51337	.43630	.37136	.31657	.27027	.23107	.19784	17
18	.83602	.70016	.58739	.49363	.41552	.35034	.29586	.25025	.21199	.17986	18
19	.82774	.68643	.57029	.47464	.39573	.33051	.27651	.23171	.19449	.16351	19
20	.81954	.67297	.55367	.45639	.37689	.31180	.25842	.21455	.17843	.14864	20
21	.81143	.65978	.53755	.43883	.35894	.29415	.24151	.19866	.16370	.13513	21
22	.80340	.64684	.52189	.42195	.34185	.27750	.22571	.18394	.15018	.12285	22
23	.79544	.63416	.50669	.40573	.32557	.26180	.21095	.17031	.13778	.11168	23
24	.78757	.62172	.49193	.39012	.31007	.24698	.19715	.15770	.12640	.10153	24
25	.77977	.60953	.47760	.37512	.29530	.23300	.18425	.14602	.11597	.09230	25

(*continued*)

N	11%	12%	13%	14%	15%	16%	17%	18%	19%	20%	N
01	0.90090	0.89286	0.88496	0.87719	0.86957	0.86207	0.85470	0.84746	0.84034	0.83333	01
02	.81162	.79719	.78315	.76947	.75614	.74316	.73051	.71818	.70616	.69444	02
03	.73119	.71178	.69305	.67497	.65752	.64066	.62437	.60863	.59342	.57870	03
04	.65873	.63552	.61332	.59208	.57175	.55229	.53365	.51579	.49867	.48225	04
05	.59345	.56743	.54276	.51937	.49718	.47611	.45611	.43711	.41905	.40188	05
06	.53464	.50663	.48032	.45559	.43233	.41044	.38984	.37043	.35214	.33490	06
07	.48166	.45235	.42506	.39964	.37594	.35383	.33320	.31392	.29592	.27908	07
08	.43393	.40388	.37616	.35056	.32690	.30503	.28478	.26604	.24867	.23257	08
09	.39092	.36061	.33288	.30751	.28426	.26295	.24340	.22546	.20897	.19381	09
10	.35218	.32197	.29459	.26974	.24718	.22668	.20804	.19106	.17560	.16151	10
11	.31728	.28748	.26070	.23662	.21494	.19542	.17781	.16192	.14756	.13459	11
12	.28584	.25667	.23071	.20756	.18691	.16846	.15197	.13722	.12400	.11216	12
13	.25751	.22917	.20416	.18207	.16253	.14523	.12989	.11629	.10420	.09346	13
14	.23199	.20462	.18068	.15971	.14133	.12520	.11102	.09855	.08757	.07789	14
15	.20900	.18270	.15989	.14010	.12289	.10793	.09489	.08352	.07359	.06491	15
16	.18829	.16312	.14150	.12289	.10686	.09304	.08110	.07078	.06184	.05409	16
17	.16963	.14564	.12522	.10780	.09293	.08021	.06932	.05998	.05196	.04507	17
18	.15282	.13004	.11081	.09456	.08080	.06914	.05925	.05083	.04367	.03756	18
19	.13768	.11611	.09806	.08295	.07026	.05961	.05064	.04308	.03669	.03130	19
20	.12403	.10367	.08678	.07276	.06110	.05139	.04328	.03651	.03084	.02608	20
21	.11174	.09256	.07680	.06383	.05313	.04430	.03699	.03094	.02591	.02174	21
22	.10067	.08264	.06796	.05599	.04620	.03819	.03162	.02622	.02178	.01811	22
23	.09069	.07379	.06014	.04911	.04017	.03292	.02702	.02222	.01830	.01509	23
24	.08170	.06588	.05322	.04308	.03493	.02838	.02310	.01883	.01538	.01258	24
25	.07361	.05882	.04710	.03779	.03038	.02447	.01974	.01596	.01292	.01048	25

(continued)

N	21%	22%	23%	24%	25%	26%	27%	28%	29%	30%	N
01	0.82645	0.81967	0.81301	0.80645	0.80000	0.79365	0.78740	0.78125	0.77519	0.76923	01
02	.68301	.67186	.66098	.65036	.64000	.62988	.62000	.61035	.60093	.59172	02
03	.56447	.55071	.53738	.52449	.51200	.49991	.48819	.47684	.46583	.45517	03
04	.46651	.45140	.43690	.42297	.40960	.39675	.38440	.37253	.36111	.35013	04
05	.38554	.37000	.35520	.34111	.32768	.31488	.30268	.29104	.27993	.26933	05
06	.31863	.30328	.28878	.27509	.26214	.24991	.23833	.22737	.21700	.20718	06
07	.26333	.24859	.23478	.22184	.20972	.19834	.18766	.17764	.16822	.15937	07
08	.21763	.20376	.19088	.17891	.16777	.15741	.14776	.13878	.13040	.12259	08
09	.17986	.16702	.15519	.14428	.13422	.12493	.11635	.10842	.10109	.09430	09
10	.14864	.13690	.12617	.11635	.10737	.09915	.09161	.08470	.07836	.07254	10
11	.12285	.11221	.10258	.09383	.08590	.07869	.07214	.06617	.06075	.05580	11
12	.10153	.09198	.08339	.07567	.06872	.06245	.05680	.05170	.04709	.04292	12
13	.08391	.07539	.06780	.06103	.05498	.04957	.04472	.04039	.03650	.03302	13
14	.06934	.06180	.05512	.04921	.04398	.03934	.03522	.03155	.02830	.02540	14
15	.05731	.05065	.04481	.03969	.03518	.03122	.02773	.02465	.02194	.01954	15
16	.04736	.04152	.03643	.03201	.02815	.02478	.02183	.01926	.01700	.01503	16
17	.03914	.03403	.02962	.02581	.02252	.01967	.01719	.01505	.01318	.01156	17
18	.03235	.02789	.02408	.02082	.01801	.01561	.01354	.01175	.01022	.00889	18
19	.02673	.02286	.01958	.01679	.01441	.01239	.01066	.00918	.00792	.00684	19
20	.02209	.01874	.01592	.01354	.01153	.00983	.00839	.00717	.00614	.00526	20
21	.01826	.01536	.01294	.01092	.00922	.00780	.00661	.00561	.00476	.00405	21
22	.01509	.01259	.01052	.00880	.00738	.00619	.00520	.00438	.00369	.00311	22
23	.01247	.01032	.00855	.00710	.00590	.00491	.00410	.00342	.00286	.00239	23
24	.01031	.00846	.00695	.00573	.00472	.00390	.00323	.00267	.00222	.00184	24
25	.00852	.00693	.00565	.00462	.00378	.00310	.00254	.00209	.00172	.00142	25

(concluded)

N	31%	32%	33%	34%	35%	36%	37%	38%	39%	40%	N
01	0.76336	0.75758	0.75188	0.74627	0.74074	0.73529	0.72993	0.72464	0.71942	0.71429	01
02	.58272	.57392	.56532	.55692	.54870	.54066	.53279	.52510	.51757	.51020	02
03	.44482	.43479	.42505	.41561	.40644	.39754	.38890	.38051	.37235	.36443	03
04	.33956	.32939	.31959	.31016	.30107	.29231	.28387	.27573	.26788	.26031	04
05	.25920	.24953	.24029	.23146	.22301	.21493	.20720	.19980	.19272	.18593	05
06	.19787	.18904	.18067	.17273	.16520	.15804	.15124	.14479	.13865	.13281	06
07	.15104	.14321	.13584	.12890	.12237	.11621	.11040	.10492	.09975	.09486	07
08	.11530	.10849	.10214	.09620	.09064	.08545	.08058	.07603	.07176	.06776	08
09	.08802	.08219	.07680	.07179	.06714	.06283	.05882	.05509	.05163	.04840	09
10	.06719	.06227	.05774	.05357	.04973	.04620	.04293	.03992	.03714	.03457	10
11	.05129	.04717	.04341	.03998	.03684	.03397	.03134	.02893	.02672	.02469	11
12	.03915	.03574	.03264	.02984	.02729	.02498	.02287	.02096	.01922	.01764	12
13	.02989	.02707	.02454	.02227	.02021	.01837	.01670	.01519	.01383	.01260	13
14	.02281	.02051	.01845	.01662	.01497	.01350	.01219	.01101	.00995	.00900	14
15	.01742	.01554	.01387	.01240	.01109	.00993	.00890	.00798	.00716	.00643	15
16	.01329	.01177	.01043	.00925	.00822	.00730	.00649	.00578	.00515	.00459	16
17	.01015	.00892	.00784	.00691	.00609	.00537	.00474	.00419	.00370	.00328	17
18	.00775	.00676	.00590	.00515	.00451	.00395	.00346	.00304	.00267	.00234	18
19	.00591	.00512	.00443	.00385	.00334	.00290	.00253	.00220	.00192	.00167	19
20	.00451	.00388	.00333	.00287	.00247	.00213	.00184	.00159	.00138	.00120	20
21	.00345	.00294	.00251	.00214	.00183	.00157	.00135	.00115	.00099	.00085	21
22	.00263	.00223	.00188	.00160	.00136	.00115	.00098	.00084	.00071	.00061	22
23	.00201	.00169	.00142	.00119	.00101	.00085	.00072	.00061	.00051	.00044	23
24	.00153	.00128	.00107	.00089	.00074	.00062	.00052	.00044	.00037	.00031	24
25	.00117	.00097	.00080	.00066	.00055	.00046	.00038	.00032	.00027	.00022	25

APPENDIX D Table 2 Present value of $1.00 received annually at the end of each year for N years.

$$A = \frac{1}{i}\left[1 - \frac{1}{(1 + i)^N}\right]$$

Year	1%	2%	3%	4%	5%	6%	7%	8%	9%	10%	Year
1	0.9901	0.9804	0.9709	0.9615	0.9524	0.9434	0.9346	0.9259	0.9174	0.9091	1
2	1.9704	1.9416	1.9135	1.8861	1.8594	1.8334	1.8080	1.7833	1.7591	1.7355	2
3	2.9410	2.8839	2.8286	2.7751	2.7232	2.6730	2.6243	2.5771	2.5313	2.4868	3
4	3.9020	3.8077	3.7171	3.6299	3.5459	3.4651	3.3872	3.3121	3.2397	3.1699	4
5	4.8535	4.7134	4.5797	4.4518	4.3295	4.2123	4.1002	3.9927	3.8896	3.7908	5
6	5.7955	5.6014	5.4172	5.2421	5.0757	4.9173	4.7665	4.6229	4.4859	4.3553	6
7	6.7282	6.4720	6.2302	6.0020	5.7863	5.5824	5.3893	5.2064	5.0329	4.8684	7
8	7.6517	7.3254	7.0196	6.7327	6.4632	6.2098	5.9713	5.7466	5.5348	5.3349	8
9	8.5661	8.1622	7.7861	7.4353	7.1078	6.8017	6.5152	6.2469	5.9852	5.7590	9
10	9.4714	8.9825	8.5302	8.1109	7.7217	7.3601	7.0236	6.7101	6.4176	6.1446	10
11	10.3677	9.7868	9.2526	8.7604	8.3064	7.8868	7.4987	7.1389	6.8052	6.4951	11
12	11.2552	10.5753	9.9539	9.3850	8.8632	8.3838	7.9427	7.5361	7.1607	6.8137	12
13	12.1338	11.3483	10.6349	9.9856	9.3935	8.8527	8.3576	7.9038	7.4869	7.1034	13
14	13.0038	12.1062	11.2960	10.5631	9.8986	9.2950	8.7454	8.2442	7.7861	7.3667	14
15	13.8651	12.8492	11.9379	11.1183	10.3796	9.7122	9.1079	8.5595	8.0607	7.6061	15
16	14.7180	13.5777	12.5610	11.6522	10.8377	10.1059	9.4466	8.8514	8.3125	7.8237	16
17	15.5624	14.2918	13.1660	12.1656	11.2740	10.4772	9.7632	9.1216	8.5436	8.0215	17
18	16.3984	14.9920	13.7534	12.6592	11.6895	10.8276	10.0591	9.3719	8.7556	8.2014	18
19	17.2261	15.6784	14.3237	13.1339	12.0853	11.1581	10.3356	9.6036	8.9501	8.3649	19
20	18.0457	16.3514	14.8774	13.5903	12.4622	11.4699	10.5940	9.8181	9.1285	8.5136	20
21	18.8571	17.0111	15.4149	14.0291	12.8211	11.7640	10.8355	10.0168	9.2922	8.6487	21
22	19.6605	17.6580	15.9368	14.4511	13.1630	12.0416	11.0612	10.2007	9.4424	8.7715	22
23	20.4559	18.2921	16.4435	14.8568	13.4885	12.3033	11.2722	10.3710	9.5802	8.8832	23
24	21.2435	18.9139	16.9355	15.2469	13.7986	12.5503	11.4693	10.5287	9.7066	8.9847	24
25	22.0233	19.5234	17.4131	15.6220	14.0939	12.7833	11.6536	10.6748	9.8226	9.0770	25

* For the derivation of A, see note following this table.

(continued)

Year	11%	12%	13%	14%	15%	16%	17%	18%	19%	20%	Year
1	0.9009	0.8929	0.8850	0.8772	0.8696	0.8621	0.8547	0.8475	0.8403	0.8333	1
2	1.7125	1.6901	1.6681	1.6467	1.6257	1.6052	1.5852	1.5656	1.5465	1.5278	2
3	2.4437	2.4018	2.3612	2.3216	2.2832	2.2459	2.2096	2.1743	2.1399	2.1065	3
4	3.1024	3.0373	2.9745	2.9137	2.8550	2.7982	2.7432	2.6901	2.6386	2.5887	4
5	3.6959	3.6048	3.5172	3.4331	3.3522	3.2743	3.1993	3.1272	3.0576	2.9906	5
6	4.2305	4.1114	3.9976	3.8887	3.7845	3.6847	3.5892	3.4976	3.4098	3.3255	6
7	4.7122	4.5638	4.4226	4.2883	4.1604	4.0386	3.9224	3.8115	3.7057	3.6046	7
8	5.1461	4.9676	4.7988	4.6389	4.4873	4.3436	4.2072	4.0776	3.9544	3.8372	8
9	5.5370	5.3282	5.1317	4.9464	4.7716	4.6065	4.4506	4.3030	4.1633	4.0310	9
10	5.8892	5.6502	5.4262	5.2161	5.0188	4.8332	4.6586	4.4941	4.3389	4.1925	10
11	6.2065	5.9377	5.6869	5.4527	5.2337	5.0286	4.8364	4.6560	4.4865	4.3271	11
12	6.4924	6.1944	5.9176	5.6603	5.4206	5.1971	4.9884	4.7932	4.6105	4.4392	12
13	6.7499	6.4235	6.1218	5.8424	5.5831	5.3423	5.1183	4.9095	4.7147	4.5327	13
14	6.9819	6.6282	6.3025	6.0021	5.7245	5.4675	5.2293	5.0081	4.8023	4.6106	14
15	7.1909	6.8109	6.4624	6.1422	5.8474	5.5755	5.3242	5.0916	4.8759	4.6755	15
16	7.3792	6.9740	6.6039	6.2651	5.9542	5.6685	5.4053	5.1624	4.9377	4.7296	16
17	7.5488	7.1196	6.7291	6.3729	6.0472	5.7487	5.4746	5.2223	4.9897	4.7746	17
18	7.7016	7.2497	6.8399	6.4674	6.1280	5.8178	5.5339	5.2732	5.0333	4.8122	18
19	7.8393	7.3658	6.9380	6.5504	6.1982	5.8775	5.5845	5.3162	5.0700	4.8435	19
20	7.9633	7.4694	7.0248	6.6231	6.2593	5.9288	5.6278	5.3527	5.1009	4.8696	20
21	8.0751	7.5620	7.1016	6.6870	6.3125	5.9731	5.6648	5.3837	5.1268	4.8913	21
22	8.1757	7.6446	7.1695	6.7429	6.3587	6.0113	5.6964	5.4099	5.1486	4.9094	22
23	8.2664	7.7184	7.2297	6.7921	6.3988	6.0442	5.7234	5.4321	5.1668	4.9245	23
24	8.3481	7.7843	7.2829	6.8351	6.4338	6.0726	5.7465	5.4509	5.1822	4.9371	24
25	8.4217	7.8431	7.3300	6.8729	6.4641	6.0971	5.7662	5.4669	5.1951	4.9476	25

139

(continued)

Year	21%	22%	23%	24%	25%	26%	27%	28%	29%	30%	Year
1	0.8264	0.8197	0.8130	0.8065	0.8000	0.7937	0.7874	0.7813	0.7752	0.7692	1
2	1.5095	1.4915	1.4740	1.4568	1.4400	1.4235	1.4074	1.3916	1.3761	1.3609	2
3	2.0739	2.0422	2.0114	1.9813	1.9520	1.9234	1.8956	1.8684	1.8420	1.8161	3
4	2.5404	2.4936	2.4483	2.4043	2.3616	2.3202	2.2800	2.2410	2.2031	2.1662	4
5	2.9260	2.8636	2.8035	2.7454	2.6893	2.6351	2.5827	2.5320	2.4830	2.4356	5
6	3.2446	3.1669	3.0923	3.0205	2.9514	2.8850	2.8210	2.7594	2.7000	2.6427	6
7	3.5079	3.4155	3.3270	3.2423	3.1611	3.0833	3.0087	2.9370	2.8682	2.8021	7
8	3.7256	3.6193	3.5179	3.4212	3.3289	3.2407	3.1564	3.0758	2.9986	2.9247	8
9	3.9054	3.7863	3.6731	3.5655	3.4631	3.3657	3.2728	3.1842	3.0997	3.0190	9
10	4.0541	3.9232	3.7993	3.6819	3.5705	3.4648	3.3644	3.2689	3.1781	3.0915	10
11	4.1769	4.0354	3.9018	3.7757	3.6564	3.5435	3.4365	3.3351	3.2388	3.1473	11
12	4.2785	4.1274	3.9852	3.8514	3.7251	3.6060	3.4933	3.3868	3.2859	3.1903	12
13	4.3624	4.2028	4.0530	3.9124	3.7801	3.6555	3.5381	3.4272	3.3224	3.2233	13
14	4.4317	4.2646	4.1082	3.9616	3.8241	3.6949	3.5733	3.4587	3.3507	3.2487	14
15	4.4890	4.3152	4.1530	4.0013	3.8593	3.7261	3.6010	3.4834	3.3726	3.2682	15
16	4.5364	4.3567	4.1894	4.0333	3.8874	3.7509	3.6228	3.5026	3.3896	3.2832	16
17	4.5755	4.3908	4.2190	4.0591	3.9099	3.7705	3.6400	3.5177	3.4028	3.2948	17
18	4.6079	4.4187	4.2431	4.0799	3.9279	3.7861	3.6536	3.5294	3.4130	3.3037	18
19	4.6346	4.4415	4.2627	4.0967	3.9424	3.7985	3.6642	3.5386	3.4210	3.3105	19
20	4.6567	4.4603	4.2786	4.1103	3.9539	3.8083	3.6726	3.5458	3.4271	3.3158	20
21	4.6750	4.4756	4.2916	4.1212	3.9631	3.8161	3.6792	3.5514	3.4319	3.3198	21
22	4.6900	4.4882	4.3021	4.1300	3.9705	3.8223	3.6844	3.5558	3.4356	3.3230	22
23	4.7025	4.4985	4.3106	4.1371	3.9764	3.8273	3.6885	3.5592	3.4384	3.3254	23
24	4.7128	4.5070	4.3176	4.1428	3.9811	3.8312	3.6918	3.5619	3.4406	3.3272	24
25	4.7213	4.5139	4.3232	4.1474	3.9849	3.8342	3.6943	3.5640	3.4423	3.3286	25

(concluded)

Year	31%	32%	33%	34%	35%	36%	37%	38%	39%	40%	Year
1	0.7634	0.7576	0.7519	0.7463	0.7407	0.7353	0.7299	0.7246	0.7194	0.7143	1
2	1.3461	1.3315	1.3172	1.3032	1.2894	1.2760	1.2627	1.2497	1.2370	1.2245	2
3	1.7909	1.7663	1.7423	1.7188	1.6959	1.6735	1.6516	1.6302	1.6093	1.5889	3
4	2.1305	2.0957	2.0618	2.0290	1.9969	1.9658	1.9355	1.9060	1.8772	1.8492	4
5	2.3897	2.3452	2.3021	2.2604	2.2200	2.1807	2.1427	2.1058	2.0699	2.0352	5
6	2.5875	2.5342	2.4828	2.4331	2.3852	2.3388	2.2939	2.2506	2.2086	2.1680	6
7	2.7386	2.6775	2.6187	2.5620	2.5075	2.4550	2.4043	2.3555	2.3083	2.2628	7
8	2.8539	2.7860	2.7208	2.6582	2.5982	2.5404	2.4849	2.4315	2.3801	2.3306	8
9	2.9419	2.8681	2.7976	2.7300	2.6653	2.6033	2.5437	2.4866	2.4317	2.3790	9
10	3.0091	2.9304	2.8553	2.7836	2.7150	2.6495	2.5867	2.5265	2.4689	2.4136	10
11	3.0604	2.9776	2.8987	2.8236	2.7519	2.6834	2.6180	2.5555	2.4956	2.4383	11
12	3.0995	3.0133	2.9314	2.8534	2.7792	2.7084	2.6409	2.5764	2.5148	2.4559	12
13	3.1294	3.0404	2.9559	2.8757	2.7994	2.7268	2.6576	2.5916	2.5286	2.4685	13
14	3.1522	3.0609	2.9744	2.8923	2.8144	2.7403	2.6698	2.6026	2.5386	2.4775	14
15	3.1696	3.0764	2.9883	2.9047	2.8255	2.7502	2.6787	2.6106	2.5457	2.4839	15
16	3.1829	3.0882	2.9987	2.9140	2.8337	2.7575	2.6852	2.6164	2.5509	2.4885	16
17	3.1931	3.0971	3.0065	2.9209	2.8398	2.7629	2.6899	2.6206	2.5546	2.4918	17
18	3.2008	3.1039	3.0124	2.9260	2.8443	2.7668	2.6934	2.6236	2.5573	2.4941	18
19	3.2067	3.1090	3.0169	2.9299	2.8476	2.7697	2.6959	2.6258	2.5592	2.4958	19
20	3.2112	3.1129	3.0202	2.9327	2.8501	2.7718	2.6977	2.6274	2.5606	2.4970	20
21	3.2147	3.1158	3.0227	2.9349	2.8519	2.7734	2.6991	2.6285	2.5616	2.4979	21
22	3.2173	3.1180	3.0246	2.9365	2.8533	2.7746	2.7000	2.6294	2.5623	2.4985	22
23	3.2193	3.1197	3.0260	2.9377	2.8543	2.7754	2.7008	2.6300	2.5628	2.4989	23
24	3.2209	3.1210	3.0271	2.9386	2.8550	2.7760	2.7013	2.6304	2.5632	2.4992	24
25	3.2220	3.1220	3.0279	2.9392	2.8556	2.7765	2.7017	2.6307	2.5634	2.4994	25

ANSWERS

CHAPTER 2

1(a) Indirect labor   (f) Direct materials
 (b) Indirect materials   (g) Direct materials
 (c) Indirect labor   (h) Indirect materials
 (d) Direct labor   (i) Indirect labor
 (e) Indirect materials

2(a) The basic charge and unlisted calls to department by instrument; calls listed by number to caller department.

(b) Relative value of department space to total value. For example:

	Rental Value	Percentage	Prorate Value, $
Factory rental in area			
Factory 20,000			
Shipping 2,000			
Office rental in area			
Administrative 3,000			
Sales 1,000			
		100%	$

(c) Prorated on volume of space (to be heated).
(d) Electricity: (1) for power to factory; (2) for lighting by wattage of fixtures in spaces.
(e) Property taxes: like rental in part (b).

(These are only suggestions; actual facts may change allocations.)

CHAPTER 3

1. *Time Attendance.* Gross wage computation is easiest for the employee to understand and easiest for the accounting department to compute, but it is unrelated to productive effort and may give the company excessive costs that the company may fail to recognize.

    Incentive wage computation, when properly designed and properly explained to the employee, will result in encouraging the employee to produce more in a given time because he can secure the immediate benefit of higher wages and the company can benefit by the reduction of per-unit conversion costs.

2. An Emerson type of efficiency plan is better than a straight piecework plan because the employee can raise the level of payment on all pieces produced as his efficiency continues to increase.

3(a) The employee deductions required by law are:
     Social Security and Medicare premiums
     Federal income taxes withheld
     State and city income taxes withheld (where applicable)
     State disability insurance premiums

 (b) The deductions themselves do not affect costs because they are taken out of the employee's gross earnings. The employee pays these taxes. However, it increases the cost of payroll preparation and adds the cost of payroll tax preparation to other accounting costs.

4(a) The employer payroll taxes required by law are:
     Social Security and Medicare premiums to match the employee contribution
     Federal and state unemployment insurance premiums
     State workmens' compensation insurance payments
     Other state or local taxes on payroll

 (b) These taxes are a cost to the employer over and above gross wages and must be absorbed by management into the cost of product via the factory overhead accounts.

5(a) Fringe benefits are given to employees because other employers are giving them and the company must meet competitive prices for labor in order to insure a good work force. Other benefits are required by law or because of union contract provisions. Some are given as a paternalistic expression on the part of the management (the Christmas turkey) or to display civic involvement (sports teams) or for other reasons.

 (b) The justification for fringe benefits is that they build employee loyalty and esprit de corps, help establish a community of interest between management and labor, etc. But here one must be careful! It hasn't always worked that way. Sometimes a fringe benefit given in an improper way has caused more ill will than if it had not been given at all. For example, if employees are not informed in advance about basic changes in benefits such as medical insurance plans, particularly when the change results in higher employee deductions, much distrust can result even when the change improves the benefit in the long run.

6. No, this is not a good plan because it does not decrease conversion costs as production increases (as Table 4.A1 shows). An incentive plan that does not decrease conversion cost per unit as production increases should be reviewed.

Table 4.A1 Question 6.

	Units Produced	Conversion Cost, $	Conversion Cost/Unit, $
A	66	85.80	1.30
C	73	91.25	1.25
E	87	78.30	0.90
D	115	109.25	0.95
B	128	128.00	1.00

CHAPTER 4

1. 364 units (52 units/day × 7 days).

2. $2,000 [($30,000 − $10,000) × 10%]

3. See Figure 4.A1.

Figure 4.A1 Question 3.

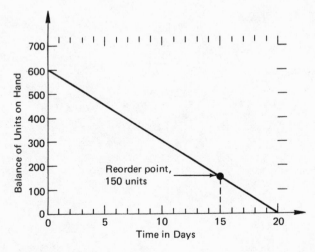

4. See Figure 4.A2.

Figure 4.A2   Question 4.

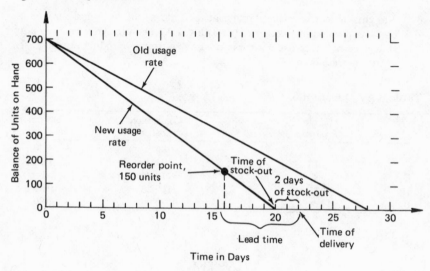

Time in Days

5.

	Last Year	Increase, %	This Year
Salaries	$200,000	5	$210,000
Fringe benefits	60,000	7	64,200
Other costs	140,000	8	151,200
Total purchase costs	$400,000		$425,400
Purchase orders processed	4,000		4,500
Purchase cost/order	$100		$95

6.

	Last Year	Change	This Year
Holding costs	$ 400,000	Up 30%	$520,000
Average inventory	$1,200,000	Less 25% and then up 10%	$990,000
Holding cost is a percentage of average inventory	33.3%		52.5%

7.   EOQ *Last Year*   EOQ *This Year*

$$\sqrt{\frac{2 \times \$100 \times 1,200}{\$25 \times 0.333}} \qquad \sqrt{\frac{2 \times \$95 \times 1,200}{\$35 \times 0.525}}$$

$$\sqrt{\frac{240,000}{8.325}} \qquad\qquad \sqrt{\frac{228,000}{18.375}}$$

$$\sqrt{28,829} \qquad\qquad\quad \sqrt{12,408}$$

$$170 \qquad\qquad\qquad\quad 111$$

CHAPTER 5

1.

Beginning inventory	$ 27,000
Purchases (net)	290,000
	317,000
Less ending inventory	32,000
Cost of materials used	$285,000

2(a) Cost of materials used:

FIFO

Jan.	500 u. @ $10			$ 5,000
Feb.	100 u. @ 10	$ 1,000		
	300 u. @ 11	3,300		4,300
Mar.	400 u. @ 11	4,400		
	300 u. @ 12	3,600		8,000
				$17,300

Average

600 u. @ $10.00	$ 6,000	
700 u. @ 11.00	7,700	
500 u. @ 12.00	6,000	
1,800 u. @ 10.94	$19,700	
Used 1,600 u. @ $10.94		$17,504

Moving Average

	Beginning inventory	600 u.	@ $10.00	$ 6,000
Jan.	Usage	500 u.		5,000
		100 u.		1,000
Feb.	Purchase	700 u.	@ 11.00	7,700
		800 u.	@ 10.88	8,700
Feb.	Usage	400 u.		4,352
		400 u.		4,348
Mar.	Purchase	500 u.	@ 12.00	6,000
		900 u.	@ 11.50	10,348
Mar.	Usage	700 u.		8,050
		200 u.		$ 2,298

Cost of materials used	Jan.	$ 5,000
	Feb.	4,352
	Mar.	8,050
		$17,402

LIFO

Jan.	500 u. @ $10		$ 5,000
Feb.	400 u. @ 11		4,400
Mar.	500 u. @ 12	$6,000	
	200 u. @ 11	2,200	8,200
			$17,600

(b) Ending inventory

Beginning inventory	600 u. @ $10.00	$ 6,000
Feb. purchase	700 u. @ 11.00	7,700
Mar. purchase	500 u. @ 12.00	6,000
Goods available		$19,700

	FIFO	Average	Moving Average	LIFO
Goods available	$19,700	$19,700	$19,700	$19,700
Inventory used	17,300	17,504	17,402	17,600
Ending inventory	$ 2,400	$ 2,196	$ 2,298	$ 2,100

Proof:

FIFO	200 u. @ $12.00 = $2,400
Average	200 u. @ $10.94 = $2,188 ($8 difference due to rounding)
Moving average	200 u. @ $11.50 = $2,300 ($2 difference due to rounding)
LIFO	100 u. @ $10.00 = $1,000
	100 u. @ $11.00 = 1,100
	$2,100

CHAPTER 6

1(a) Profits are less by $50,000.

(b) Burden rate before the computer:

$$\frac{\$1,400,000}{\$600,000} = \$2.333/\text{direct labor dollar}$$

Burden rate after the computer:

$$\frac{\$1,450,000}{\$600,000} = \$2.417/\text{direct labor dollar}$$

(c)

	Before Computer	After Computer
Direct materials ($500,000/100,000 u.)	$ 5.000	$ 5.000
Direct labor ($600,000/100,000 u.)	6.000	6.000
Factory overhead (6.000 × $2.333)	13.998	
(6.000 × $2.417)		14.502
	$24.998	$25.502

The per-unit cost increased by $0.504 (2.02%).

2. Firm profitability should increase.

In reviewing the position descriptions of all indirect personnel, it might be developed that some responsibilities are assigned to more than one person (involving additional cost due to duplication of effort, confusion in the lower echelon of the company as to who is in fact responsible, and the possibility that each of the persons assigned the responsibility assumes the other is doing it so it doesn't get done at all) and that some responsibilities have been assigned to no one.

In performing the management audit there is the possibility that the procedures in effect can be improved, that the cost of the function is greater than the benefits received, and that certain persons are not effectively contributing to the company.

3. The average individual should be able to measure the quantity of material in a simple ($25) product and cost it out within a reasonable range. He should also be able to tell what labor is involved in making the product and cost this out within a reasonable range. That is because he has the product in hand. However, the factory overhead is made up of factory indirect wages, utilities, insurance, etc., which can vary widely from plant to plant and locality to locality. The age of the plant may affect depreciation charges. The quality of administration and plant support may vary widely from one company to another. Therefore, this cost is much more difficult to assess, and even an approximate range might not be easy to develop without seeing the factory and looking at its books.

4(a)

$$\frac{\$43,000 - \$3,000}{10 \text{ years}} = \$4,000/\text{year expense}$$

(b)

$$\frac{100\%}{10 \text{ years}} = 10\%/\text{year}$$

$$10\% \times 150\% = 15\%$$

		Depreciation Expense	Accumulated Depreciation
Year 1	$43,000 × 15%	$6,450	$ 6,450
Year 2	($43,000 − $6,450) × 15%	5,483	11,933
Year 3	($43,000 − $11,933) × 15%	4,660	16,593

(c)

$$10 + 9 + 8 + 7 + 6 + 5 + 4 + 3 + 2 + 1 = 55$$

Year 1 $40,000 × 10/55 = $7,273
Year 2 $40,000 × 9/55 = 6,545
Year 3 $40,000 × 8/55 = 5,818

5. $$\frac{\$190,000}{50,000 \text{ DLH}} = \$3.80/\text{DLH}$$

6. $120,000 × 150% = $180,000

7(a) Sum-of-the-years' digits because it has the greatest expense in these two years.

(b) Compare declining balance and sum-of-the-years' digits to straight-line depreciation.

(c)

	Income Tax Savings in Year 1	Year 2
Straight-line	-0-	-0-
Declining balance	$12,690	$ 7,614
Sum-of-the-years' digits	17,301	13,458

CHAPTER 7

1. No, fixed costs are not always the same over the total range of production. They are called fixed to distinguish them from the variable costs and to simplify the explanation of break-even analysis.

2. Contribution margin analysis is another way of viewing the cost-volume-profit relationship. It compares sales price per unit to variable cost per unit to obtain contribution margin per unit.

3. Break-even point is the level of production and sales where sales income equals total costs or where no profits or losses are generated.

4. (Sales price/unit) $\times Q =$ fixed costs $+$ (variable cost/unit) $\times Q$
    ($240,000/40,000 u.) $\times Q =$ \$40,000 $+$ ($160,000/40,000 u.) $\times Q$
    $6Q$ $=$ \$40,000 $+$ $4Q$
    $2Q$ $=$ \$40,000
    Q $=$ 20,000 units

5. Contribution margin = \$7.00/unit − \$4.00/unit = \$3.00/unit. Therefore,

$$\text{BEQ} = \frac{\text{fixed costs}}{\text{contributions margin}} = \frac{\$15,000}{\$3.00/\text{unit}} = 5,000 \text{ units}$$

6. See Figure 7.A1.

Figure 7.A1 Question 6.

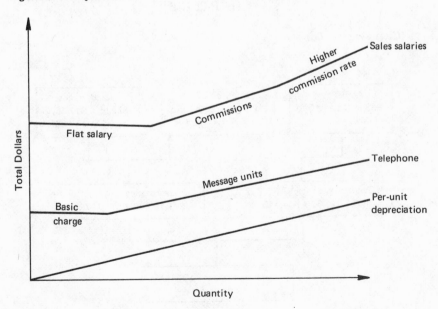

7.

Product	Sales in Units	Sales Price/ Unit	Total Sales	Variable Cost/ Unit	Total Variable Cost	Direct Labor Hours to Produce 1 Unit	Total Direct Labor Hours
A	20,000	$15.00	$300,000	$ 7.50	$150,000	4	80,000
B	15,000	10.00	150,000	7.00	105,000	2	30,000
C	10,000	20.00	200,000	16.00	160,000	3	30,000
Total			$650,000		$415,000		140,000

$$\text{Composite sales price/DLH } \frac{\$650,000}{140,000 \text{ DLH}} = \$4.643/\text{DLH}$$

$$\text{Composite variable cost/DLH } \frac{\$415,000}{140,000 \text{ DLH}} = \$2.964/\text{DLH}$$

$$\text{Composite contribution margin} = \$1.679/\text{DLH}$$

$$\text{Break-even quantity} = \frac{\$125,000}{\$1.679/\text{DLH}} = 74,449 \text{ DLH}$$

CHAPTER 8

1. Changing units first:

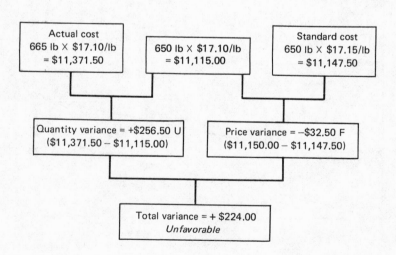

Changing price first:

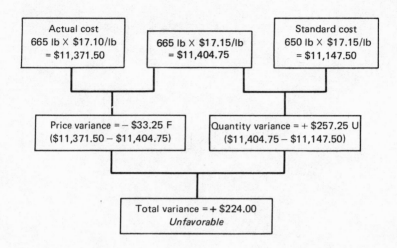

Proof: $11,371.50 − $11,147.50 = $224.00 unfavorable

2.

	Hours	Wage Rate, $/hr	Total Wages
Smith	20.2	3.50	$ 70.700
Spade	14.3	3.75	53.625
Jackson	22.7	3.80	86.260
Harold	15.8	3.85	60.830
Total	73.0		$271.415

Average hourly wage = $3.718.

Changing hours first:

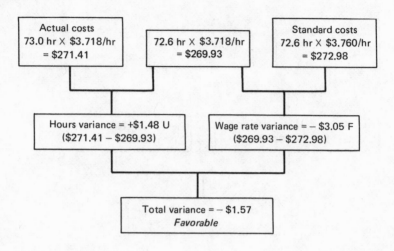

Changing wage rate first:

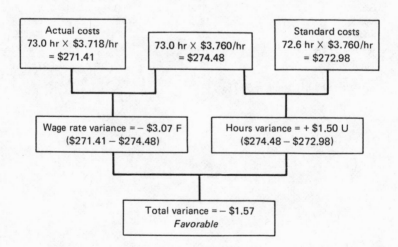

CHAPTER 10

1. Budget cost at 240,000 units $172,000
   Budget cost at 256,000 units
   [($189,000 − $180,000) × (6/10)] + $180,000   185,400

   Budget variance unfavorable $ 13,400

2. Price/unit @ $5.00 for 8,300 units $41,500
   Price/unit @ $5.10 for 8,300 units   42,330

   Price variance unfavorable $ 830

3(a) Budget cost at 82,000 units
     (4,700 units @ $6.50) $30,550.00
     Budget cost at 79,000 units
     {[(4,500 − 3,750) × (9/10)] + (3,750)} @ $6.50   28,762.50

     Budget variance favorable $ 1,787.50

     Price/unit @ $6.50 for 4,400 units $28,600.00
     Price/unit @ $6.60 for 4,400 units   29,040.00

     Price variance unfavorable $ 440.00

     Units at "normal efficiency"
     [(4,500 − 3,750) × (9/10)] + 3,750   4,425
     Units actually used   4,400

     Units saved favorable   25

                    25 u. @ $6.50 $162.50

     Total variance
     Budget variance favorable $1,787.50
     Price variance unfavorable   440.00
     Efficiency variance favorable   162.50

     Total variance $1,510.00

     Proof: Budgeted for 82,000 units
             (4,700 @ $6.50) $30,550.00
             Actual cost (4,400 @ $6.60)   29,040.00

             Total variance $ 1,510.00

Index